Plough Quar

BREAKING GROUND FOR A RENE\

Winter 2020, Number 23

Editor's Letter	Peter Mommsen	3
Readers Respond		6
Family and Friends	Chris Hoke and Editors	10
Family Corner: One Inch off the Ground	Maureen Swinger	12

Feature: Cities

Reading: The Pilgrim City	Saint Augustine	15
Re-Mapping Belfast	Jenny McCartney	16
Interview: Serving Kings	James Macklin with Jason Storbakken	27
Up Hill	Adriano Cirino	32
Digging Deeper	Susannah Black	43
Reading: Beneath the Tree of Life	N. T. Wright	45
City of Bones, City of Graces	Joseph Bottum	48
Building Community in Pittsburgh	Brandon McGinley	58
In the Valley of Lemons	Jose Corpas	63
Reading: The Sidewalk Ballet	Jane Jacobs	66
City of Clubs	Clare Coffey	68

Poetry

Christmas Reading	Richard Crashaw	14
The Eternal City	Philip Britts	54
Visual Poem: Those Winter Sundays	Julian Peters	79

Reviews and Profiles

Review: *This City Is Killing Me*	John Thornton Jr.	84
Editors' Picks		89
Reading: Not Just Personal	Eberhard Arnold	91
Forerunners: Madeleine Delbrêl	Jason Landsel	96

Artists: Gail Brodholt, Michelangelo Buonarroti, Ben Ibebe, Brian Peterson, Chota, Raphael, Gertrude Hermes, Valentino Belloni, Tony Taj, Aristarkh Lentulov

Meet the community behind *Plough*

Plough Quarterly is published by the Bruderhof, an international community of families and singles seeking to follow Jesus together. Members of the Bruderhof are committed to a way of radical discipleship in the spirit of the Sermon on the Mount. Inspired by the first church in Jerusalem (Acts 2 and 4), they renounce private property and share everything in common in a life of nonviolence, justice, and service to neighbors near and far. The community includes people from a wide range of backgrounds. There are twenty-three Bruderhof settlements in both rural and urban locations in the United States, England, Germany, Australia, Paraguay, and South Korea, with around 3,000 people in all. To learn more or arrange a visit, see the community's website at *bruderhof.com*.

Plough Quarterly features original stories, ideas, and culture to inspire everyday faith and action. Starting from the conviction that the teachings and example of Jesus can transform and renew our world, we aim to apply them to all aspects of life, seeking common ground with all people of goodwill regardless of creed. The goal of *Plough Quarterly* is to build a living network of readers, contributors, and practitioners so that, in the words of Hebrews, we may "spur one another on toward love and good deeds." *Plough Quarterly* includes contributions that we believe are worthy of our readers' consideration, whether or not we fully agree with them. Views expressed by contributors are their own and do not necessarily reflect the editorial position of *Plough* or of the Bruderhof communities.

Editor: Peter Mommsen. Senior Editors: Veery Huleatt, Sam Hine. Editor-at-Large: Caitrin Keiper. Managing Editor: Shana Goodwin. Associate Editors: Susannah Black, Maureen Swinger, Ian Barth. International Editions: Daniel Hug (German), Chungyon Won (Korean), Allen Page (French). Designers: Rosalind Stevenson, Miriam Burleson. Creative Director: Clare Stober. Copy Editors: Wilma Mommsen, Mary Catherine Ausman. Fact Checker: Emmy Barth Maendel. Marketing Director: Trevor Wiser.
Founding Editor: Eberhard Arnold (1883–1935)

Plough Quarterly No. 23: Cities
Published by Plough Publishing House, ISBN 978-0-87486-339-0
Copyright © 2020 by Plough Publishing House. All rights reserved.

Scripture quotations (unless otherwise noted) are from the New Revised Standard Version Bible, copyright © 1989 the Division of Christian Education of the National Council of the Churches of Christ in the United States of America. Used by permission. All rights reserved.
Front cover: Gail Brodholt, *London Calling*; image used with permission. Back cover: Aristarkh Lentulov, *The gate with a tower. New Jerusalem*, image from WikiArt (public domain). Richard Bauckham quotation from *The Theology of the Book of Revelation* (Cambridge University, 1993).
Inside front cover: Ben Ibebe, *Urban Series (Neighborhood)*; image used with permission.

Editorial Office	Subscriber Services	United Kingdom	Australia
151 Bowne Drive	PO Box 345	Brightling Road	4188 Gwydir Highway
Walden, NY 12586	Congers, NY 10920-0345	Robertsbridge	Elsmore, NSW
T: 845.572.3455	T: 800.521.8011	TN32 5DR	2360 Australia
info@plough.com	subscriptions@plough.com	T: +44(0)1580.883.344	T: +61(0)2.6723.2213

Plough Quarterly (ISSN 2372-2584) is published quarterly by Plough Publishing House, PO Box 398, Walden, NY 12586. Individual subscription $32 / £24 / €28 per year. Subscribers outside the United Kingdom and European Union pay in US dollars. Periodicals postage paid at Walden, NY 12586 and at additional mailing offices.
POSTMASTER: Send address changes to *Plough Quarterly*, PO Box 345, Congers, NY 10920-0345.

STATEMENT OF OWNERSHIP, MANAGEMENT, AND CIRCULATION (Required by 39 U.S.C. 3685) 1. Title of publication: Plough Quarterly. 2. Publication No: 0001-6584. 3. Date of filing: October 1, 2019. 4. Frequency of issue: Quarterly. 5. Number of issues published annually: 4. 6. Annual subscription price: $32.00. 7. Complete mailing address of known office of publication: Plough Quarterly, P.O. Box 398, Walden, NY 12586. 8. Same. 9. Publisher: Plough Publishing House, same address. Editor: Peter Mommsen, same address. Managing Editor: Sam Hine, same address. 10. Owner: Plough Publishing House, P.o. Box 398, Walden, NY 12586. 11. Known bondholders, mortgages, and other securities: None. 12. The purpose, function, and nonprofit status of this organization and the exempt status for federal income tax purposes has not changed during preceding 12 months. 13. Publication Title: Plough Quarterly. 14. Issue date for circulation data below: Fall 2018–Summer 2019. 15. Extent and nature of circulation: Average No. copies of each issue during preceding 12 months: A. Total number of copies (net press run)—15,250. B.1. Mailed outside-county paid subscriptions: 8,106. B.2. Mailed in-county paid subscriptions: 0. B.3. Paid distribution outside the mails including sales through dealers and carriers, street vendors, counter sales, and other non-USPS paid distribution: 115. B.4. Other classes mailed through the USPS: 0. C. Total paid distribution: 8,221. D.1. Free distribution by mail: Outside-county—1,732. D.2. In-county—0. D.3. Other classes mailed through the USPS—0. Free distribution outside the mail—1,833. E. Total free distribution: 3,565. F. Total Distribution: 11,785. G. Copies not distributed: 3,465. H. Total: 15,250. I. Percent paid—69.76%. Actual No. copies of single issue published nearest to filing date: A. 14,000. B.1. 7,013. B.2. 0. B.3. 31. B.4. 0. C. 7,044. D.1. 1,709. D.2. 0. D.3. 0. D.4. 1,859. E. 3,568. F. 10,612. G. 3,388. H. 14,000. I. 66.38%. Electronic copy circulation: Average No. copies of each issue during preceding 12 months: A. Total No. Electronic Copies: 172. B. Total paid print copies plus paid electronic copies: 8,393. C. Total print distribution plus paid electronic copies: 11,957. D. Percent paid: 70.19%. Actual No. copies of single issue published nearest to filing date: A. 182. B. 7,226. C. 10,794. D. 66.94%. 17. Publication of Statement of Ownership: Winter 2020. 18. I certify that the statements made by me above are correct and complete. Sam Hine, Editor, October 1, 2019.

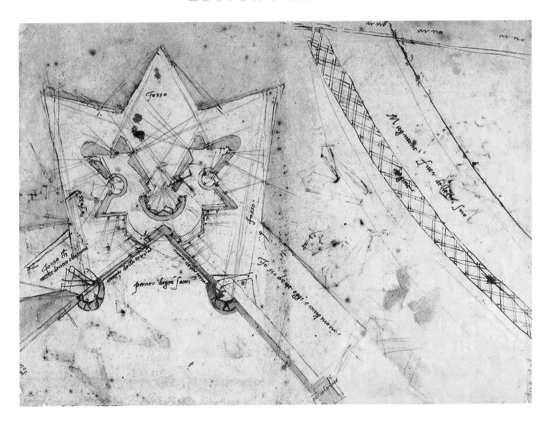

In Search of a City

PETER MOMMSEN

Dear Reader,

I T MIGHT SEEM A BAD MOVE for a magazine named after a farm tool to bring out an issue on cities. Especially if that magazine is published by an Anabaptist community that originated in a back-to-the-land movement and still has the whiff of hayfield and woodlot to it. Why not stick to what you're good at? Why jump lanes?

Because the future of humanity, pretty clearly, is urban. It's a well-known tale, yet the numbers still astound: In 1800, just 7 percent of the world's population lived in cities. By 1900,

that figure was 16 percent, today it's 55 percent, and by 2050 it's projected to reach 68 percent, with one-third of the growth occurring in India, China, and Nigeria alone, according to a 2018 United Nations report. Each week, three million people move from the country to cities. Urbanization is arguably the biggest change of habitat that our species has ever undergone. It's bound to change us.

For anyone who cares about the common good of humanity, then, cities need to matter. This applies all the more to Christians, who are called not only to love their neighbors as themselves, but to "go into all the world"

Michelangelo Buonarroti, *Study for Porto San Gallo,* 1525

(Mark 16:15). Increasingly, that world is made up of cities.

An urban world calls for an urban Christianity. Pastors such as Tim Keller of New York City's Redeemer Presbyterian Church or Les Isaac of London's Street Pastors have found new ways of building church community in a city environment, combining an orthodox faith with open-minded outreach. The Bruderhof, too, despite its agrarian origins, has started around a dozen urban communities since 2003, with houses in Peckham, London; Harlem, New York; St. Petersburg, Florida; Asunción, Paraguay; and Brisbane, Australia. Other branches of the universal church can point to diverse examples of such urban community-building.

Enthusiasm for the city runs especially high among younger evangelical Christians, a group that still mostly hails from the heartland and the suburbs. An earlier generation of evangelicals thrilled to the challenge of mission in Asia or Africa; today, the adventure is in urban church planting. Books on the theology of the city abound, bearing titles like *The Urban Christian* and replete with scriptural arguments supporting a preferential option for the city. They've popularized a new set of terms such as "incarnational mission" – the idea that simply being present as Christians in an urban neighborhood, "without an agenda," can serve as a witness to the love of Christ.

Unsurprisingly, such attempts don't always hit the mark, any more than last century's missions did. Earnest church planters can allow their good intentions to outstrip their self-awareness. A long-term resident of a minority neighborhood told me of a group of middle-class white twenty-somethings who discerned a calling to move in to practice a "ministry of presence." "Actually," he commented, "Jesus has been present here all along, way before they arrived." He appreciated the newcomers' desire for radical discipleship, but reckoned they'd eventually see that they were less likely to catalyze mission than to receive it.

The modern city is an electrifying concentration of creativity, energy, and cultural dynamism. And it's also still the "cauldron of unholy loves" that Saint Augustine discovered in Carthage one and a half millennia ago. It's the place where the cruelties of mammon, the hubris of power, and the perversions of lust manifest themselves most crassly. That's why even Keller warns Christians of the dangers of "loving the city": be careful what it is that you love. As the poet William Blake, walking through London in 1794, put it:

> I wander thro' each charter'd street,
> Near where the charter'd Thames does flow.
> And mark in every face I meet
> Marks of weakness, marks of woe. . . .
>
> How the Chimney-sweepers cry
> Every blackning Church appalls,
> And the hapless Soldiers sigh
> Runs in blood down Palace walls
>
> But most thro' midnight streets I hear
> How the youthful Harlots curse
> Blasts the new-born Infants tear
> And blights with plagues
>   the Marriage hearse

> **The city is preeminently the place where man fulfills God's original mandate to create culture and community.**

Sexual exploitation, callous militarism, false religion, legalized greed: in the city, Blake diagnoses the symptoms of the demonic.

Yet ugliness is not the city's only face. The city, not the country, is where Plato wrote his dialogues, Dante the *Divine Comedy*, and Shakespeare his *Lear*. In the city Bach composed the *Saint Matthew Passion*, Handel the *Messiah*, and Coltrane *A Love Supreme*. The city is the place of Chartres Cathedral and the Hagia Sophia, of the Medina of Marrakesh and Central Park. It's preeminently the place where man fulfills God's original mandate to create culture and community (Gen. 1:28).

To the Christian church especially, the city has given birth to remarkable movements of revival and renewal. In the United States, these include the Christian Community Development movement started by civil rights pioneers John and Vera Mae Perkins, based on the "three Rs": relocation, reconciliation, and redistribution. The generation before saw the founding of the Catholic Worker movement by Dorothy Day and Peter Maurin. Before them came the settlement houses such as Hull House in Chicago and Kingsley Hall in London, as well as Toyohiko Kagawa's cooperatives in the slums of Tokyo and William and Catherine Booth's Salvation Army. The history extends still earlier to the thirteenth century, to the houses for the poor established by the Beguines and Beghards in the Low Countries and by

Saint Elizabeth of Hungary in central Europe. It goes back to the birth of the church itself: as scholars such as Wayne Meeks and Alan Kreider have shown, early Christianity was largely an urban movement.

It's in that spirit that we've assembled this issue of *Plough*. A few highlights: James Macklin tells about one of Manhattan's oldest faith institutions serving the homeless, The Bowery Mission, which this year celebrates its 140th anniversary (page 27). Brandon McGinley describes how a few families have become more intentional about community in a Pittsburgh neighborhood (page 58). Jenny McCartney writes of the hard work for reconciliation in her native Belfast (page 16), while Jose Corpas recounts one woman's fight to establish schools in a Guatemala barrio (page 63).

Finally, as N. T. Wright reminds us (page 45), the story of Scripture culminates not in a return to the green paradise of Eden, but in a city: the New Jerusalem. It's a city that will be both a temple and a garden, over which will tower the Tree of Life (Rev. 22). It's a city where – since swords are to be beaten into plowshares – farm tools will not be out of place.

Warm greetings,

Peter

Peter Mommsen
Editor

Michelangelo Buonarroti, *Plan for a Church,* ca. 1560

"Love, and Do What You Will"

On Will Willimon's "The Unchosen Calling,"
Autumn 2019: As a Catholic priest, I'm grateful
for this article's attempt to address modernity's
approach to faith as a means of personal fulfillment. Willimon argues, "Christians assert
the un-American conviction that our lives are
less interesting than the God who assigns us."
Our attention to God should inform every
choice, not just the choices we call "ethical."
God entered our human life fully and calls us
to enter his life fully. This runs up against the
modern dictate that we own ourselves, that we
have made ourselves.

It's true that vocation is God's calling, and
not "your bundle of need and desire." I hesitate,
though, to entirely reject desires and talents in
the vocational decision. They are themselves
part of God's gifts to us; they are themselves
responsive to what God does in us.

As Augustine tells us, everyone is drawn by
his own delight, and part of what Augustine
realizes in the *Confessions* is that these delights
are themselves changed and shaped by God.
The modern problem with the idea of vocation
is not just its subjectivity, its quest to find what
might fulfill us by introspection into "what
I truly desire," but also an unwillingness to
consider how changeable we and our desires
really are. The problem then lies in sorting out
which of our desires are good, and which are
an invitation to chase after the wind.

This same dynamic applies in all questions
of ethics. Modernity sees the fulfillment of
desire as the final aim of the human life.
Humans should be free to fulfill those desires,
so long as they don't prevent anyone else from
doing so, or cause harm. We're individual
units, occasionally in proximity to each other;
we're free to the extent that we're able to move
about without colliding in an objectionable
way against other similar units.

But this isn't reality. We don't believe this
vision of humanity, because we recognize the
sovereignty of God over even our desires, and
we recognize those desires as only part of a
relationship with God and with each other.
We are members of the natural societies of
family and polity, with their corresponding
loves and obligations, and it's as such members
that God deals with us. He deals with us, too,
as those called to play a role in the building
up of another society, the church, the body of
Christ – and that church is charged, finally,
with this task of discerning where each of us fit
in this great work.

Augustine pointed out that what made
actions good or bad was whether they were
done in love or hatred. And so he says "love
and do what you will." But we human beings
are extremely good at self-deception and can
convince ourselves falsely that this or that
action is genuinely loving. The love Augustine
had in mind was not our achievement, but our
full participation in a love which is prior and
superior to us: the love of God for us, shown
in sending his Son into the world that we may
have life, and loving us in all our unlovability
in order to make us able to love.

Father Robert Krishna OP, Chaplain,
Monash University, Melbourne, Australia

Vision from Inside

On Pola Rader's "Icon and Mirror," Autumn
2019: Among the otherwise excellent
articles in this issue, the "Portfolio" entitled
"Icon and Mirror – A photo-essay on the
women of Voronezh, Russia" sticks out
like a disappointing sore thumb. I write as
a communicant of the Russian Orthodox
Church (ROC), traveling to Russia regularly,
including Voronezh, and with contacts in
church circles in that city.

---

*We welcome letters to the editor. Letters may be edited for length and clarity, and may be published
in any medium. They should be sent with the writer's name and address to* letters @plough.com.

You can tell any story you want with a few well-shot photographs. In Russian this is known as a Potemkin village, named after the fake villages built to inspire the empress traveling past. I fear that the text and photos of "Icon and Mirror" together build such a village.

Your article asks: "Can the voice of modern Orthodox women be heard in the church today?" Whatever these women told your reporter, my answer is "no." Yes, they can work as bookkeepers, or running social services: they do a lot of the drudge work. But official decision-making in the ROC remains an entirely male prerogative. This is probably a main reason why the Russian church right now is fast losing its drawing power among the better educated, "modern" classes, and in particular among women. Those not bound to the system, as are the priests' wives featured in the article, are moving out to the periphery.

Yes, Russian women can be formidable and strong, with a long history of holding the fort in difficult national and family situations – war, alcoholism, exile – where men have failed. But do these women draw their strength from their Orthodox faith, or simply from an ancestral Russian understanding of womanhood? My money's on the latter.

On reading the article, my Voronezh correspondent quoted to me the Russian saying "Don't expect to see the inside of people's coats on the first visit." This was very clearly a first visit.   *Michael Lomax, Brussels*

Pola Rader responds: "Can the voice of modern Orthodox women be heard in the church today?" This question is very important to me. But I didn't let myself give an unambiguous answer to it in my photo-essay; otherwise, the essay would have been trivial.

It was important to me to make readers, and viewers, think about this topic, and I am pleased to see that Mr. Lomax was not left indifferent. Many of the things that he writes in criticism are not papered over in the article; the issue is complex. However, this was no first impression, and I did not encounter Voronezh as a Potemkin village. I have spent a great deal of time in Voronezh, as a child and a teenager; I returned there for the project with that background. And I am, myself, a modern Orthodox woman.

Visions from outside are often very superficial, although I don't say that they are necessarily wrong. But it was important for me to catch and share the vision from inside, and at least by means of my photo-essay to let the voice of the modern Orthodox woman be heard, and to show her face.

A Common Inheritance

On Plough Quarterly No. 21: Beyond Capitalism, *Summer 2019:* I enjoyed each article in this issue, from Hart's indictment of capitalism to Boyle's move off the grid.

A challenge is to integrate these views with the observation that markets and capitalism are the means which God has chosen to bless women and men materially. There is plenty of historical and current evidence of results from other systems. Without developed markets, life for most of us would be short and brutal. Experiments with other systems, even the Bruderhof's Community Playthings as described by John Rhodes, thrive in good part because they are surrounded by a wealthy, market-capitalist system.

Perhaps a point of integration relates to David Bentley Hart's contention that "Whatever else capitalism may be, it is first and foremost a system for producing as much *private* wealth as possible by squandering as much as possible of humanity's *common* inheritance of the goods of creation." And Hart is consistent with Brandon Terry's article on Martin Luther King Jr.: "In

1967 . . . King demanded that we ask 'Who owns the oil?' or 'Who owns the iron ore?'" Both points imply that we hold a common inheritance, God-given, to bless all members of a society. The blessing is developed by shared activity which, from observation, has been most effectively coordinated by markets, and on a large scale by capitalism.

Common inheritance energizes thinking about the common good – to be overseen by good governance. I sense that *Plough* authors have more to share about how we might explore governance in new ways.

Larry A. Smith, President,
ScholarLeaders International

For many years I've read the German edition of *Plough*. The new format has increased the effectiveness of its outreach; contributions have become more extensive and helpful. The latest issue has given me real enthusiasm; we in Europe are currently in a heated discussion about values. Globalized capitalism and the principles of market liberalism create unacceptable living conditions for ordinary people. But the left-green alternatives being offered strike many of us as inadequate, especially here in eastern Germany, a region that endured forty years of socialist experimentation.

Unfortunately, I don't belong to a Christian community like the Bruderhof, so in a sense I am the young man of Matthew 19, trapped in material and family ties – but who still hopes for God's grace according to verse 26. A Christian life beyond capitalism and socialism is also possible in a living church or a stable gathering of households under the Word of God. As Peter Mommsen wrote in the editorial: "While a new generation is asking critical questions about justice, solidarity and . . . happiness, we Christians should not forget that we had access to the answers all the time."

Steffen Grahnert, Dresden, Germany

As one who enjoys the challenges of *Plough*, I was left disturbed by the most recent edition, *Beyond Capitalism*, not so much by the obvious dangers of capitalism, but by the implication that only a communal approach, like that of the Bruderhof, was a genuine response to money and property.

My previous contacts with your communities in northern New South Wales have been generous, whereas the tone of this recent issue is otherwise. There are millions of believers who, agreeing about the dangers of money, property, and capitalism, are seeking to genuinely use their possessions to bring glory to God and the good to others.

Scripture has other, more positive things to say about private property. We need not divest ourselves of property to be disciples. Consider Acts 5:4, the 8th Commandment's endorsement of private property, our Lord's word in Acts 20:35, and the witness of the believers who had homes large enough for the churches to meet and sufficient wealth to support the church's needy. It is true that the rich young ruler went away from Jesus because he would not part with the money he loved, but our Lord commended Zacchaeus in the next chapter when he made restitution without giving away all his wealth.

Jesus' diagnosis of the human condition is far more radical than your articles suggest (Luke 12:13–21). Greed is possible for all of us, rich or poor, and can only be dealt with by a true conversion of the heart. The overrealized eschatology proposed by David Bentley Hart fails to account for the sin that causes both communism and capitalism to fail to perfectly deliver the equality, justice, and generosity that believers expect to be fully realized only at Jesus' return. Hence the exhortations to eschew greed and the love of money (Col. 3:5, 1 Tim. 6:9–10) and to use the money and possessions entrusted to us with radical Christ-like generosity (2 Cor. 8:1–9, 1 Tim. 6:17–19). These may enable us to meet the needs of others (Gal. 6:9–10), rescue us from greed, and prove to be the salt that saves human systems from banditry (Mat. 5:13–16).

The problem, so well presented, demands of disciples a serious response, attractive and consistent with the full range of biblical example and expectation. Whether sought in community or in the world, both demand mutual respect and a balanced reading of scripture. *Peter Brain, Perth, Australia*

Peter Mommsen responds: I thank Peter Brain for his candid letter regarding our *Beyond Capitalism* issue, and am glad to reassure him that *Plough* does not believe that only the Bruderhof's way of life is a "genuine response to money and property." That would be absurd; Christ's church is far greater than that, thank God. As my editorial mentioned, over the last two millennia the church has brought forth a rich variety of movements that practiced economic sharing inspired by the New Testament, many very different from my own community. The broad spectrum of traditions represented on *Plough*'s pages illustrates this diversity.

Let's set aside for a moment the specific characteristics of the Bruderhof, one movement among many in the stream of church history. The question remains: is there any "genuine [Christian] response to money and property" that is not in some way communal? The New Testament is not as accommodating of private property as often supposed. The apostles' writings, and above all the Christ's words in the Gospels, say virtually nothing about a right to private ownership, and a great deal about giving up riches and sharing one's possessions in fraternal love. As the biblical scholar Richard Hays summarizes: "While the particular mandates and forms of expression may vary, the New Testament witnesses speak

Young fan: a photograph sent in by a *Plough* reader

loudly in chorus: the accumulation of wealth is antithetical to serving God's kingdom, and Jesus' disciples are called at least to share their goods generously with those in need, and perhaps even to give everything away in order to follow him more freely. . . . For the church to heed the New Testament's challenge on the question of possessions would require nothing less than a new Reformation" (*The Moral Vision of the New Testament*, 467–468).

To prescribe this or that form of sharing possessions would be presumptuous, and Brain is absolutely right that we must not go beyond Scripture. Yet isn't the more common danger to duck the issue? In the end, each would-be disciple must reckon with how to live out the Master's startling and unqualified call (Luke 14:33): "None of you can become my disciple if you do not give up all your possessions."

Honor, Money, and War

On Scott Beauchamp's "Mercenaries Out of the Gate," Autumn 2019: This article has two theses that I'm not sure are related by logic, as opposed to sentiment. The first is that the military and capitalism share a metastasizing impulse, "unyoked from any moral principles." The second is that modern mercenaries are more "honest" servants of an amoral military than are "typical" soldiers like Beauchamp.

(Continued on page 94)

Dealing in Resurrection

Chris Hoke

When our small band of jail chaplains north of Seattle considered starting a direct-trade coffee-roasting business to support incarcerated gang members reentering society, the first man who wanted in was a tall, tattooed former white supremacist.

His addiction before prison had led to his trade as a meth cook. Roasting coffee, he shrugged, couldn't be that much harder. *Hey,* we thought, *transferrable skills?*

That's been our passion at Underground Coffee ever since.

Take the woman who graduated from a Christian drug recovery home and then approached us for a job. She didn't have a good work history on paper, and confessed to having been a mid-level drug dealer in our area. Now, two years into working with us, she runs the accounts and bookkeeping for Fidalgo Coffee Roasters, the larger company operating Underground Coffee. She's a natural with numbers. She closed all open accounts within a week.

Another man covered in gang-related tattoos used to drive all over our valley hustling doctors for pill subscriptions. At Underground Coffee, he now supports his recovery and his family as the delivery van driver, crisscrossing three counties each day, charming grocery store and café owners and often upping sales with each conversation.

It's more than giving those with criminal convictions a charitable chance at a job. We've found that those rising out of our society's underground of drug dealing and addiction have countless transferrable skills that can transform our businesses.

Underground Coffee, now a partnership between Underground Ministries and Fidalgo Coffee Roasters, is creating a culture that celebrates employment as a key to interrupting recidivism and a sign of resurrection.

How can you support us? Well, churches and offices consume a lot of coffee. Some might call it an addiction. We want to be your dealer.

Hit us up.

To learn more, visit underground.coffee.

Faces of Santa Ana

See Brian Peterson's artwork on pages 84–88.

Sitting in his living room one night four years ago, Brian Peterson heard the screams of a man on the street below. Two days later Peterson, a car designer for Kia Motors who had recently moved to California with his wife, Vanessa, found himself sitting by that man on the sidewalk and asking him for permission to paint his portrait.

Dozens of portraits later, Peterson's nonprofit, Faces of Santa Ana, is changing lives and growing rapidly. The basic process: Peterson befriends a person experiencing homelessness, paints his or her portrait, and puts fifty percent of the proceeds from the painting's sale into a "love account," to be used however the subject wishes: for food, medicine, or art projects. While helping those in need, the project also inspires those who purchase the artwork. Peterson says, "They're investing in a life, in someone who is living and breathing and hoping and looking for love and looking for change." In some cases, the painting's subject and purchaser develop a lasting friendship.

More recently, Peterson's work has expanded to creating murals and involving local high school students in painting portraits; the nonprofit has been spreading to other cities as well. In November, Peterson resigned from his job to pursue Faces of Santa Ana full time. Support the project at *facesofsantaana.com*.

Orders of Magnitude

Sister Andrea and Sister Roseann are an order of two. But the vitality of the Sisters of the Gospel of Life in Glasgow makes up for their small numbers. Both women found

Brian Peterson working on a portrait

their vocation caring for the needs of women with unexpected pregnancies who want an alternative to abortion. Since 2000, the two nuns have lived in full Christian community, sharing a life of prayer and running a center that provides counseling and practical support for such women.

Though several others have considered a vocation with this order, the sisters are still waiting for someone to join them. This has not discouraged them, they say. As they continue to advocate for women, network with others doing similar work, and witness to the possibility of radical Christian community, they remind themselves of Jesus' promise, "Where two or three are gathered in my name, I am there among them." ⤳

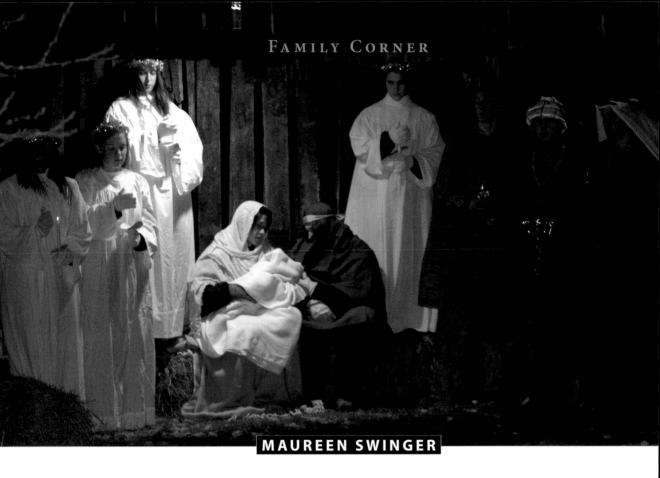

MAUREEN SWINGER

One Inch off the Ground

A child meets her guardian angel at a live nativity

A live nativity scene at a Bruderhof community

"**M**OM, WHY DOES NOBODY ELSE in my class know the name of their guardian angel?" She's at it again – the five-year-old with the unanswerable questions. She's never been puzzled for a moment as to the identity of her angel. He's her "Uncle D" – whom she has never met, unless you count two years of hangout time (supposing you measure time at all, up there) before her birth and after his death.

I did not give her the idea. But I have told the kids countless stories about my brother Duane, who never spoke or walked, but lived thirty-one years and lived them well. Our family's

hearts were shaped around him, and we were so accustomed to one-way conversations that I often find myself talking to him in my head still, with a sense that he's quite close, tilting his chin and quietly listening. That's not just because of the photo on the living room wall.

I'm aware that we small humans can never understand the world of angels – great, inscrutable beings created before our time. Still, not only the child beside me, but the child within clings to the idea that God takes care of guardian angel duties in the here and now. And he might just delegate an uncle to watch out for a small niece with a penchant for accidents.

Maureen Swinger is an editor at Plough. *She lives at the Fox Hill Bruderhof in Walden, New York.*

Duane was no stranger to accidents. He had severe seizures all his life, and no level of precaution spared him his share of tumbles, bumps, and chipped teeth. Who better to keep an eye on a child who in her first two years managed to rack up a concussion, a choking episode, and a tooth chipped into a triangle reminiscent of a klutzy baby vampire? Her equally adventurous brother and sister have managed to reach tween-hood without any natural disasters. This one – she needs eyes on her. And she knows they're there.

When I tuck her into bed, she says good night to me and then to any angels who might be in the room, starting with Uncle D. On the way to kindergarten, she talks about how the sky ends one inch off the ground, so our angels can fly along next to us. A golden winter sunset means D and crew are baking Christmas cookies. (Maybe he's baking them – not sure if he's eating them. He wouldn't let anything sweet pass his lips back when I knew him.) It never bothered her that she couldn't see him, and she never expected to – until last Christmas Eve, when she did.

The live nativity was out under the stars that night, with a steady wind flickering the candle flames. Our entire community stood in silence before a shabby stable, listening to the Christmas story. My little girl's head kept turning from the well-swaddled baby, snoozing in Mary's arms, to a tall, dark-haired angel standing just outside the stable, with a big torch that flared in the wind. As we began filing past the tableau, singing carols and sheltering our candles, she suddenly tugged me out of the line. "I think that's Uncle D," she said, her eyes outshining the candles. "Please, Mom, can we go and ask him?"

I felt my heart thud. On the holiest night of the year, adults know that we stand before a beautiful symbol. What a time for a child to find out too. I tried to formulate a reason why we should not approach the angel. If she saw Duane, I saw a high-school student who had recently moved to our community. But I could not say no to those eyes.

He was a very tall angel; we both had to look up. She tugged at my skirt. "Ask him, Mom!" she whispered, not taking her eyes off his face. I didn't see that I had a choice. With an apologetic smile, I muttered: "My daughter wants to know if you are her Uncle D." Between the wind and the singing, how could he understand such an obscure question? But I guess angels can hear into a child's heart. He smiled down at her and said, "Yes."

The author's brother Duane, 1980–2011

The child glowed. She stood and beamed at him until the singing crowd jostled us onward. Away from the torches, our candles snuffed out, it was pitch dark and bitterly cold. She didn't notice. I didn't care.

She didn't say anything till bedtime. As I tucked the quilt up around her chin, she gave me a sleepy smile and said, "Isn't it nice that it was his turn to guard baby Jesus this year?"

She didn't need to see him to know that angels are real. And I'm not worried about what will happen when she's old enough to realize that the nativity figures on Christmas Eve are people she knows and loves here on earth. That moment comes for all of us, along with the deeper knowledge that God is still with us, all around us, one inch off the ground.

Before I went to sleep, my thoughts went out to thank the young man who said yes to a child on Christmas night. But I ended up thanking my brother. ⇥

Raphael, *Study of Heads, Mother and Child*, 1509

From "In the Holy Nativity of Our Lord"

Gloomy night embraced the place
    Where the Noble Infant lay;
The Babe looked up and showed his face,
    In spite of darkness, it was day.
It was thy day, Sweet! and did rise
Not from the east, but from thine eyes.

We saw thee in thy balmy nest,
    Young dawn of our eternal day!
We saw thine eyes break from their east
    And chase the trembling shades away.
We saw thee, and we blessed the sight,
We saw thee by thine own sweet light.

Welcome, all wonders in one sight!
    Eternity shut in a span;
Summer in winter; day in night;
    Heaven in earth, and God in man.
Great little one, whose all-embracing birth
Lifts earth to heaven, stoops heaven to earth.

RICHARD CRASHAW (1612–1649)

Gertrude
Hermes,
*Pilgrim's
Progress*,
woodcut

READING

The Pilgrim City

AUGUSTINE OF HIPPO

TWO LOVES, THEN, have made two cities. Love of self, even to the point of contempt for God, made the earthly city, and love of God, even to the point of contempt for self, made the heavenly city. Thus the former glories in itself, and the latter glories in the Lord. The former seeks its glory from men, but the latter finds its highest glory in God, the witness of our conscience. The former lifts up its head in its own glory; the latter says to its God, *My glory, and the one who lifts up my head* (Ps. 3:3). In the former the lust for domination dominates both its princes and the nations that it subjugates; in the latter both leaders and followers serve one another in love, the leaders by their counsel, the followers by their obedience. The former loves its own strength, displayed in its men of power; the latter says to its God, *I love you, O Lord, my strength* (Ps. 18:1).

THE EARTHLY CITY, which does not live by faith, seeks an earthly peace, and it establishes a concord of command and obedience among its citizens in order to bring about a kind of accommodation among human wills with regard to the things that pertain to this mortal life. And the heavenly city – or rather, that part of it which is on pilgrimage in this mortal existence and which lives by faith – must of necessity make use of this peace as well, at least until this mortal existence, for which such peace is necessary, passes away. . . .

So long as this heavenly city is a pilgrim on earth, then, it calls forth citizens from all peoples and gathers together a pilgrim society of all languages. It cares nothing about any differences in the manners, laws, and institutions by which earthly peace is achieved or maintained. But it does not rescind or abolish any of these; rather, it preserves and follows them, provided only that they do not interfere with the religion which teaches that we are to worship the one supreme and true God, for, however different they may be in different nations, they all aim at one and the same thing – earthly peace. Thus, even the heavenly city makes use of earthly peace during its pilgrimage. ⤳

Source: William Babcock, trans. *The City of God (De Civitate Dei) XI–XXII* (New City, 2013) 136–137, 375.

Plough Quarterly • *Winter 2020*

15

In a city crisscrossed with security walls, James Moyna teaches school-children to give friendship across boundaries.

RE-MAPPING BELFAST

JENNY McCARTNEY

WHEN I WAS A CHILD in Northern Ireland, the awareness of violence suffused our daily lives. The year 1981 began in bloodshed: A Catholic Republican Socialist, Bernadette McAliskey, and her husband were attacked in their home by loyalist gunmen. An elderly Protestant Unionist, Sir Norman Stronge, and his only son were shot dead in retaliation by an Irish Republican Army (IRA) gang who then burned their house to the ground.

Spring brought the onset of the hunger strikes, which were to radicalize nationalist Ireland. A number of IRA prisoners vowed to starve themselves to death unless the British government agreed to their demands for political status in jail. The first man to go on hunger strike was Bobby Sands. A month into his fast, he was elected to parliament as a member of the Sinn Féin party. The following month, he became the first of ten hunger strikers to die that year. In Belfast, the news was accompanied by riots.

Jenny McCartney is a Belfast-born journalist and author living in London. Her recent novel, The Ghost Factory, *was published in March 2019.*

EVERYONE, REPUBLICAN OR OTHERWISE HAS THEIR OWN PARTICULAR ROLE TO PLAY

...OUR REVENGE WILL BE THE LAUGHTER OF OUR CHILDREN

Bobby Sands MP
POET, GAEILGEOIR, REVOLUTIONARY, IRA VOLUNTEER.

Republican mural of Bobby Sands, IRA prisoner and hunger striker, on the Falls Road, West Belfast

I was in my final year of primary school in South Belfast. Most of the children at my school were Protestant. I don't recall much talk about politics there, but in this instance the wider anxiety seeped into our conversation. One worried boy said that for the next few months it would surely be safer not to go into the center of town. He had probably heard this from his parents, mindful of recent IRA firebomb attacks on shops. But I remember thinking that it didn't make sense. How on earth could you not go into town? My family lived outside Belfast, but my father worked in the city center, and he drove us children across town to school.

At the same time, over in West Belfast, a seven-year-old Catholic boy named James Moyna was being drawn into the riots, excited as well as frightened. One day when the police fired plastic bullets to disperse the crowd, he jumped to avoid one skittering toward him, and it hit an elderly lady on the ankle. He felt guilty that it hadn't hit him.

Everyone in Northern Ireland at that time carried personalized maps in their heads – of where it might be safe for them to go, or where they were most likely to come under threat. The young Moyna, for example, would never stray into the nearby Protestant heartland of the Shankill Road. For him, Protestants were represented by the divisive figure of the Reverend Ian Paisley, ranting against Catholicism on the television.

But these territorial maps, even when carefully observed, didn't always keep people safe. Belfast had a way of unleashing random shocks upon its citizens. People might find themselves unwittingly standing too close to a car bomb meant for the security forces, or in a bus station or pub at exactly the wrong time.

And then there was the deepest instinct of paramilitarism, to plant an unease so profound that even the safe places were no longer safe, psychologically or otherwise. The Ulster Volunteer Force (UVF) and the Ulster Defence Association (UDA) murdered civilians in drive-by shootings in Catholic streets and homes; in the early 1970s, Moyna's mother and grandmother had been "burned out" of their house three times. The IRA often performed its targeted assassinations by simply ringing a doorbell and shooting the householder. Cars zipped around the city, delivering death. "We know where you live" was a dark threat that echoed through the conflict. It meant that the map of danger included home.

I N THAT SUMMER OF 1981, however, something happened to redraw James Moyna's map. He was selected by the Euro-Children charity to spend the summer with a German family. Father Robert Matthieu, a Belgian priest, designed the program to give disadvantaged Belfast schoolchildren – mainly from Catholic backgrounds – a break from the Troubles.

The lively Moyna was suddenly placed in a very different environment from his crowded, terraced family home. He found himself staying with the Heinz family: Heino and Gabi and their two young sons, who were close to him in age.

It was disorienting, Moyna recalls: "There was no police, no army on the street. The family was wealthy and living in all that space,

with lots of bathrooms. Back home we paid the neighbors to use their bath because we didn't have one yet." There were plays and tennis and horseback riding. There was a language barrier – "they immediately set about teaching me German" – and a different worldview.

Along with his suitcase, one of the things that Moyna brought with him to Germany was a hearty dislike of Protestants. Gabi Heinz explained to him that Protestants didn't have to be bad people. In her eagerness to convince him, she mentioned a number of friendly Protestant neighbors who had come to visit him and whose children he had often played with. Moyna listened very attentively to the names. The next day, he pitched a stone through the window of every family she had mentioned.

But in time, with patience and generosity, Moyna's hosts opened his own window on a wider, suddenly vivid world. Away from home, he began to appreciate what the Belfast-born poet Louis MacNeice meant when he wrote that the "world is crazier and more of it than we think / incorrigibly plural." Moyna returned summer after summer, even accompanying the Heinz family on trips to other parts of Europe. "The lens through which I saw life was changed."

He pitched a stone through the window of every family she had mentioned.

Back home in Belfast, there was still some cause for wariness. He remembers one Good Friday in particular: "I said to my mother, 'What's for tea?' And she said 'brown fish.' And I hated brown fish, so I went out and I joined a cross-community peace walk from Clonard Monastery." Along the way, the peace walkers ran into a notorious loyalist firebrand named George Seawright, "yelling at the top of his voice, 'You got into the Shankill, but you'll not get out!'" Seawright would later be shot dead on the Shankill by republican paramilitaries, in 1987. But on that day his words struck fear into the eleven-year-old Moyna: "I ran back home. I was never as grateful to eat brown fish in my life."

At the same time, however, other factors were changing Moyna's sense of Belfast's geography. In his first year at his Christian Brothers' secondary school, he was given the chance to take up the flute. "I had already been playing Irish traditional music on the tin whistle. I brought [the flute] home, and I assembled it and could actually play it."

His flute teacher, Miss Bolger, was a Protestant and a member of the renowned 39th Old Boys Flute Band, which had produced the world-famous flutist James Galway, who occasionally dropped back in for rehearsals. Noting Moyna's ability, Bolger invited him to come along to band rehearsals, and twice a week he traveled to the Protestant Donegall Pass for flute practice. Moyna went on to join the City of Belfast Youth Orchestra, and Clonard Monastery made a room available where he and his Protestant friends from the orchestra could play music undisturbed. Music was a different conversation, one with the power to blur the city's dividing lines.

Only 7 percent of Northern Ireland pupils go to schools that are officially integrated.

TODAY, MOYNA IS FORTY-FIVE, and a teacher at St. Bernard's Primary School in East Belfast, where he leads the "shared education project" in conjunction with two other local primary schools, Cregagh and Lisnasharragh. The pupils of St. Bernard's are predominantly Catholic, and those of the other two schools are mainly Protestant.

For a set number of days per term, the classes from P4 up to P7 – with children aged roughly from seven to eleven – are mingled. The special topic that the schools have agreed on for these lessons is information and communications technology, which can involve everything from coding and constructing a drone to script-writing and digitally animating a play.

In each classroom, there is a mix of red and blue sweaters; small heads are bent studiously over iPads as the children work on graphic design images of Northern Irish landmarks such as the hexagonal rocks of the Giant's Causeway and Samson and Goliath, the massive yellow gantry cranes of Harland and Wolff shipyard that loom over the complicated city.

There are currently sixty thousand young people involved in shared education in six hundred schools across Northern Ireland. Because this mingling of Catholic and Protestant children is primarily based on shared lessons and activities, it lacks the clunky self-consciousness of some "integrated" initiatives of the past.

Paul Smyth, a youth worker since the early 1980s, remembers numerous projects that ranged from "woeful" to "really quite good." In his early work with the Peace People, they would take cross-community groups to Norway and have "some really meaningful conversations." But he also recalls a friend's Catholic daughters being flummoxed by a bizarre day in which Protestant pupils were ushered into their school hall and seated on the opposite side from the Catholic pupils, after which there was Irish dancing on stage and someone read a poem. The two groups never actually mixed.

He laughs as he recalls a recent episode of the hit television comedy *Derry Girls,* set in Northern Ireland in the mid-1990s, which satirized an old-style exercise in reconciliation. In the show, a matinee-idol young priest attempts to lead the Catholic convent school girls and some visiting Protestant boys in a rather contrived discussion of their similarities during a residential weekend. But the teenagers – clad in "FRIENDS ACROSS THE BARRICADES" T-shirts – can only manage to come up with differences, and before long the blackboard is crammed with their examples: "Catholics really buzz off statues." "Protestants hate ABBA." "Catholic gravy is all Bisto." "Protestants love soup."

The episode was a great hit in Northern Ireland and beyond. The Irish writer Marian Keyes jokily professed herself outraged at "the slur on Catholic gravy." Protestant ABBA fans made humorous protests, including that of a flute band from Banbridge, which put out a Facebook statement publicly naming two of its band members as "fans of the Swedish singing sensations." The show's writer, Lisa McGee, who is from a Derry Catholic background, made it clear that the ABBA suggestion was not her personal view but that of a character, the reliably dippy Orla McCool.

It was a reminder that – when circumstances allow – the "two communities" do have one definite thing in common: they like a laugh. There is a particular, familiar texture to conversation in Belfast, a quickness to the banter, that is one of the things I miss when I'm away.

WHEN THE PROTESTANT CHILDREN visit St. Bernard's, they walk past a large picture of Pope Francis just inside the front doorway. If it ever did strike them as unusual, it doesn't seem to now. I ask if they found the school different at all when

James Moyna teaching a "shared education" class mingling Catholic and Protestant children from three local primary schools

WE SEEK
NOTHING BUT
THE ELEMENTARY
RIGHT IMPLANTED
IN EVERY MAN:
THE RIGHT
IF YOU ARE ATTACKED,
TO DEFEND YOURSELF.

An Ulster Volunteer Force loyalist paramilitary mural on the Newtownards Road, East Belfast

they first arrived and one girl says, "I kept getting lost!"

Religion is not uppermost in the minds of these children. They nod when Moyna asks them if they know that their schools are mainly divided between Catholic and Protestant, as are the majority of schools in Northern Ireland. It's the legacy of a system whereby the Catholic Church runs its own, state-funded "maintained" schools, with separate teacher training. Alongside them run the "controlled" state-funded schools, which are open to pupils of all faiths and none, and in practice are two-thirds Protestant. While there is often more mixing at the secondary-school level, only 7 percent of Northern Ireland pupils go to schools that are officially integrated.

Paul Close, the project coordinator for shared education, says that it isn't only about bringing together children of different backgrounds, but also teachers. Close himself had little contact with Protestants his own age until he attended a university in London and "ended up living with two lads from Larne. We discussed many times that we would probably never have met" in the home country they all share.

If an active effort had not been made to bring these children together, their early lives might never have converged either. As well as being mainly educated in separate primary schools, these children have a tendency to stick closely to the streets immediately near school and home, and Protestant and Catholic areas are marked out by commonly understood boundaries.

Moyna says of the St. Bernard's children, "Our children never walked up the Cregagh Road. And the Cregagh children wouldn't have known where St. Bernard's was, because that's not somewhere they would play or explore."

"Would you now say hello if you saw each other outside school?" Moyna asks his class.

"Yes," they all agree.

One boy from Cregagh tells me, "I play football with boys from Lisnasharragh" – the other Protestant primary. But then he adds, "I have lots of Catholic friends."

David Heggarty, the headmaster of Cregagh, is himself a former pupil. He did not meet Catholics his own age until he was a teenager, when the Royal Ulster Constabulary organized a cross-community hill walk. He and Philip Monks, the Lisnasharragh headmaster, both like how the program shares teaching skills and resources across the three schools. Parents look favorably on it, too. Research indicates a positive "attitudinal shift" in youth who have been involved.

"We're neighbors," Heggarty says. "There's a hope that the children will bump into each other at the GP's [doctor's office] or the leisure center and say hello. The little friendships that have sparked up have a real bit of depth to them."

Heggarty also notes that the Protestant Cregagh neighborhood has lately become home to a number of Catholic immigrants from Eastern Europe. In modern Belfast, immigration – predominantly Polish – is now gently complicating the historic Catholic-Protestant, Irish-British religious and cultural divides.

HAD A MAP, TOO. I was born in Belfast, but when I was six years old my family moved out to a leafy suburb. We had a detached house with a large garden, and the streets around it were calm. I was lucky to live there.

Still, there was unease. My father was a barrister who, in the early 1980s, also entered Unionist politics. The IRA had a very broad range of "legitimate targets," the phrase which it regularly used to describe anyone it felt positive about killing. That category included Unionist politicians, one of whom, a young law lecturer named Edgar Graham, was shot dead in Queen's University, opposite my school.

I began to take mental note of the statements offered to justify killing. The loyalist paramilitaries were more overtly sectarian, making it clear that, while they would rather kill Irish republicans, any Catholic was a potential target. They argued that striking random horror into the wider Catholic community would result in nationalist pressure on the IRA to cease its campaign. The theory was as strategically wrong as it was morally appalling.

> **I began to take mental note of the statements offered to justify killing.**

The IRA and the Irish National Liberation Army preferred to argue that their killing was political rather than sectarian, but in reality "political" seemed to mean that they could kill whomever they wanted. And numerous IRA atrocities were explicitly sectarian – among them the 1976 Kingsmill massacre, in which gunmen ordered eleven Protestant workmen out of their minibus and shot them, and the 1993 Shankill Road bomb, which killed Protestants queuing to buy fish. Down near the Irish border, there was a long and relentless IRA campaign to eliminate Protestants from border farms and villages and drive families further back into nearby towns.

Both republican and loyalist paramilitaries called themselves "defenders" of their communities. To have any credibility as a "defender," one needs an "attacker." In a curious way, each group relied on the other in order to survive.

My map did not contain suspicion of Catholics in general: we had Catholic relatives and friends. But it did include a deep apprehension of Irish republicans – not because they wanted a united Ireland, but because they supported killing those who thought differently. Republican strongholds in Belfast, such as the Falls Road, felt fenced-off accordingly.

Wire cages still shield the houses from potential attack.

It wasn't that I didn't think there were good people there, who were opposed to sectarian violence. It was just that if you happened to encounter someone who was for violence, and to whom your specific background might turn out to be of interest, there generally wasn't much the nonviolent people could do about it.

When the ceasefires were declared, I was in my early twenties and living in London, working as a newspaper reporter. From 1995 onward, I was frequently sent back to Belfast to cover events.

Times had changed. I went to the Falls Road for the first time. I covered the first-ever Sinn Féin rally to take place in Belfast's Ulster Hall – a symbolic event at a site where Unionists had famously rallied in opposition to Home Rule.

Gerry Kelly, an IRA bomber and hunger striker turned Sinn Féin politician, swept in to wild applause. There was a striking display of Irish dancing from a troupe of young girls, applauded by party leaders Gerry Adams and Martin McGuinness with avuncular approval from the stage. I could sense the communal excitement, the heavy tug of belonging. The excitement, however, did not include me. Although I was with other reporters, I felt on edge. I did not put money in the collection box that was emphatically passed around. I hoped that no one would notice.

Reporters from other places were free to look upon the Northern Ireland story as the fascinating, if depressing, jostling of two political tribes. But those from Northern Ireland carried our personal history with us on assignments. The *Guardian* reporter Henry McDonald, a Catholic from Belfast, had as a child narrowly survived a UVF bomb planted just outside his home. McDonald recently described how he traveled "gripped by fear" to interview the UVF leadership in 1993, one of the edgiest years. As a nervy icebreaker, he told them the story of the bomb, and one replied with a snigger, "Sorry, son. It was nothing personal."

Yet the suffering that such groups caused could not have been more personal. Each new attack left its legacy of pain and rage.

N GOOD FRIDAY, 1998, the Belfast Agreement brought an official end to the Troubles. Many hoped that with the ceasefires, the divisions between people would naturally start to heal. The international media moved on. And yet, twenty-one years later, the healing in Northern Ireland does not seem to have taken place.

At one level, Belfast has been transformed. The city center is crammed with new boutiques and coffee shops. The Cathedral Quarter is packed with restaurants and strung with fairy lights, and the sleek Europa hotel is no longer the most-bombed hotel in Europe.

But politics remains split along sectarian lines, even more so than during the worst of the violence. The center ground has

disintegrated, with power concentrated in the parties that were formerly at the extremes. Voters fear shifting position in general elections, in case their community is flattened by the other side. The delicately negotiated Stormont government collapsed in January 2017, and has not sat since.

While Stormont has been empty, the streets have been busy. The paramilitaries, including "dissident" republicans such as the New IRA and the loyalist UVF and UDA, have consolidated control in their areas. They are active in criminality and drug-dealing as well as influential in politics. Both sides have been publicly flexing their muscles with veiled or open threats of violence in negotiations over aspects of Brexit. There is a very low conviction rate for the perpetrators of regular paramilitary shootings and beatings within communities – witnesses are, understandably, reluctant to give evidence.

Against the hope that a younger generation would move decisively away from the cruelty of the past, a minority choose to celebrate it. For some who don't fully remember the reality, it has already become "radical chic." Nostalgic visions of the conflict, fed by unrepentant paramilitary commemorations, help create new victims: when the stellar young journalist Lyra McKee was killed by a New IRA bullet at a riot in Derry last April, it felt as if the worst of the old Northern Ireland had reared up to destroy the best of the new – and yet most of the rioters were younger than McKee.

In West and North Belfast, territories are heavily demarcated by the "peace walls." Since 1998, such gates, fences, and barriers have proliferated. There are now ninety-seven such mini-partitions in Belfast alone, "protecting" small communities from one another. At night, certain gates that are open during the day are locked up, as the city seals tight its little cantons.

An aerial view of one of the "peace walls" separating Protestant and Catholic communities in Belfast. Many of the barriers are opened to allow some access during the day and locked at night.

Back in Belfast, I take an informal drive with James Moyna around the peace walls. Along the way, we take in the Shankill and the Falls. Near where Moyna grew up, wire cages still shield the houses from potential attack.

The "Troubles Tour" has become a thriving local industry, whereby Belfast parades its dysfunction for visiting tourists. The murals are a form of advertising, part of the extended battle over who tells the official story. Republican murals have been gradually altered to phase out blatantly violent representations, and instead depict the IRA campaign as a natural bedfellow to selected international struggles such as those in Palestine, Cuba, Catalonia, and anti-apartheid South Africa. The loyalist walls, however, often favor brutal depictions of balaclava-clad gunmen, although there are also historical and cultural murals and a montage of the Queen.

Friendship meant a different, stronger kind of giving.

Every year, Belfast loyalists build huge, teetering bonfires to set alight on the eve of their July 12th commemorations of the 1690 victory of the Protestant King William of Orange's forces over those of the Catholic King James II. Since 1998, these constructions have grown steadily bigger. Each one is intricately pieced together to a great height, displaying melancholy remnants of the engineering talent that the builders' forefathers once put to use in Belfast shipyards. Yet these edifices don't sail forth to the rest of the world. Adorned with effigies of loyalism's opponents, they burn down to ash.

Belfast itself doesn't burn, but it smolders.

THERE IS ANOTHER STORY in Northern Ireland, too often untold. It is lived by all the people who persistently tried – and still do try – to write a better map.

One of the most heartbreaking incidents of the Troubles happened in 1998, when the Loyalist Volunteer Force, a splinter group not on ceasefire, shot dead two men in the Armagh village of Poyntzpass. The pair were drinking together in the Railway Bar, and their sectarian killers assumed that both were Catholic. But Philip Allen was Protestant. His Catholic friend Damien Trainor was going to be best man at his wedding.

The horror of the killings went around the world. But perhaps we should think longer on their deep friendship, and so many other friendships that quietly defied the oppressive logic of the Troubles. The language of the conflict centered on taking: paramilitaries took up arms, took control of areas, and then took lives. To their members, giving meant giving way and giving up.

Yet friendship meant a different, stronger kind of giving. Friendship altered Moyna's vision from that of a child who hated Protestants – and steered him away from the dangerous path down which such feelings might have led him in Troubles-era Belfast. He thinks often, he says, of the various adults who offered him chances without expecting any guarantees of reward – the Heinz family, who welcomed in a strange child from a beleaguered city, and the local teachers and musicians of both backgrounds who encouraged his musical talent and provided a context for it to mature.

"These people were my guardian angels," says Moyna. "People who gave."

Serve like you are serving a King. The Bowery Mission

AN INTERVIEW WITH JAMES MACKLIN

Serving Kings

The Bowery Mission in Manhattan at 140 Years

A s New York City's oldest street, the Bowery has long been a magnet for gangsters, hucksters, and hobos. Even today, it is still often the end of the road for homeless war veterans, released felons, people dealing with drug addiction, and others down on their luck.

For one hundred and forty years, Christians of every stripe have come together at The Bowery Mission to offer meals, hot showers, clean beds, and warm clothes.

Over the years, the Mission has helped thousands of homeless people get off the streets and back on their feet.

In a new book published by *Plough*, Jason Storbakken, a Bowery Mission director, retraces that colorful history. *Plough* asked him to catch up with James Macklin, who first passed through The Bowery Mission's iconic red doors as a homeless man over three decades ago and is now its director of outreach.

Thanksgiving dinner servers

Jason Storbakken: James, can you tell us something about your life?

James Macklin: I was born in Virginia in 1939. My teenage mother put me up for adoption. I was taken into a good home, but my adoptive mother died when I was nine, and I was bumped from one foster home to the next until I found myself on my own at age thirteen.

Since early childhood, I expressed my feelings through song, so I tried to earn a living on the Chitlin Circuit – venues where black entertainers were able to perform during the Jim Crow era. When I couldn't make ends meet, I joined seasonal workers harvesting cotton and tobacco.

How did you end up on the streets?
I experimented with gambling, alcohol, and marijuana, but it was cocaine that got me hooked, and I began hustling to feed my habit. After years of this lifestyle, I took a job and started saving money, striving to change my ways. I opened my own office-cleaning business, and believed I had conquered my addictions. Temptation surrounded me, however, and this time crack was my downfall. My business toppled, and by 1987 I was adrift on the streets of New York.

How did you find your way to The Bowery Mission?
Sleeping on the subway one night, I woke up to hear a woman's voice saying, "What's a man like you doing in a place like this?" I opened my eyes to see a white-haired lady holding out a card that offered a meal at The Bowery Mission. Since I was famished, I took the card and followed its directions. And I've been there ever since. That was the beginning of a new life. I entered and completed the recovery program and was hired as a Bowery security guard. Three years later, I was promoted to operations manager, and eventually to assistant director.

What's your role at the Mission now?
Director of Outreach, slash, slash, slash, slash. Whatever comes up. I wear a lot of hats.

From Fanny Crosby to you, there is a long history of music at The Bowery Mission. Tell us a bit about your calling as a musical minister.

Yes, I do a little singing. I'm getting a little older now – I'll soon be eighty years old – but I still got a note or two left. I used to have a group, Resurrected Beyond Belief, that would travel around the country.

During the 1980s and 90s, the Mission housed a women's program at 227 Bowery. (It later moved uptown.) These women attended the Mission's Sunday service, which is how I met Debra, who later joined my musical tours. I would sing, and Debra would share her testimony. In 1995 we were married at The Bowery Mission.

I still do a little singing. I'm going to sing tonight, one song: "Jesus, Keep Me Near the Cross." That's my favorite closing hymn.

What have you learned about the life of Christ through your experience at the Mission?
I've learned too much to tell you in this interview. But I can tell you being there I've learned a lot; I've learned more from the men than I think they would ever learn from me. I'm still learning – you stop learning when you're no longer here. What I know today, you could put it in the thimble the old ladies used to use to sew garments. But I've learned how to love people, through finding out it's impossible to serve people who you don't love.

How has the Mission changed since you first walked through those red doors over thirty years ago?
Well, when I got there, there was a tremendous discipleship program. Today we have many programs. But discipleship is still the answer. You know, you can call them students, you

can call them whatever, but we should all be disciples of Christ, learning to get our lives back together and serve him.

What's something that has not changed?
I'm beginning to hope and believe that the Mission is built on soup and salvation: feeding the hungry, clothing the naked, visiting the sick. That's what Jesus would do. You can name them programs what you want to, get all fancy, but changed lives is what matters to me.

How has homelessness changed?
Well, the drugs of choice have changed tremendously. And it's causing a lot of mental illness. When you are sleeping on the street and from boxcar to boxcar to trolley car to trolley car, you know, you lose your sanity. God didn't create us to live in the street. So that causes a lot of it. Anyway, we have a lot of mental illness that we have to deal with today. It comes in all forms. And then on top of all that there are the addictions that we suffer.

Recently a young man experiencing homelessness murdered four others as they slept down on the Bowery and in Chinatown. We had a memorial service at the Mission. A lot of people are grieving and trying to figure out homelessness. Is there some kind of meaning or message we can find from this tragedy?
Nobody wants to talk about that book called Revelation, but in the eighteenth chapter of that book all of that is described. It's really the end time. It's a shame that a man can't go to sleep, with nowhere to go in the richest city in the world, and has to be murdered without even knowing what happened. We ought to take a look at ourselves. I think it's a rude awakening in our neighborhood; I think everybody's concerned. But it shows you that The Bowery Mission still cares about people, not only in their life but even in their death.

You've maintained a long friendship and collaboration with the Bruderhof communities.

Thanksgiving Dinner at The Bowery Mission

The Bowery Mission's singing group, Resurrected Beyond Belief (James Macklin pointing)

Yes, we've worked together closely for thirty years. Several men who found a new life at The Bowery Mission went on to serve in the Bruderhof. One was Rubén Ayala – he and I graduated from the Bowery program together. He went to the Bruderhof and I stayed here. Larry Mason was another; he was the operations manager at the time. I couldn't stand the guy at first, but we learned to get along. Larry used to walk around with khaki pants on like he was still in Vietnam, and he ran the Mission with a military attitude. He had a long pony tail that hung down his back. It was Larry Mason and Rex Duval who started the big Thanksgiving celebration for the homeless at The Bowery Mission, back in 1986.

Another of your hats is a ministry with the Amish and Mennonite communities. How did that come about?

There was a gentleman at the Mission by the name of Willie Lawson when I got there, a white gentleman from Tennessee, who could have become a professional baseball player but he was out quail hunting and he had some of his fingers shot off, so that ended that. He introduced me to the Mennonites long ago. When I first met them, their first question to me was had I ever been married. I passed that test and ever since that day, I have been a member of the family. It was more recently I became a friend of the Amish. I had been told that if I got to know them I'd always be blessed, because they'll always be in your corner. And I've found that to be true. I've been blessed beyond compare.

Where does all the food come from to feed almost a thousand people a day?

Well, at one time nigh on 60 percent came from Lancaster, Pennsylvania. I guess it's still up around that figure. But we've improved upon the giving situation, with Whole Foods and Trader Joe's and a host of restaurants around the city. I think if you look at the figures you'd wonder how we do it – three meals a day, free to anybody who comes through the red doors. I've been there thirty-three years and I have never ever seen a time when we couldn't feed our people – not a single day.

What's your favorite meal when you're down at the Bowery?

Well, I'll tell you the truth, I'm sorta strict with my diet. I'm a picky eater. But there are times when I can go down there and find myself a good old piece of fried chicken. And I can always eat because Whole Foods gives us stuff that has shelf life and I can eat the fruits and veggies. I don't eat the lobster – we get those kinds of things but I don't eat them. The Mission is not just a soup kitchen; we have a variety of food. Whole Foods and Trader Joe's have really changed the way we diet at the Mission.

What's the motto of the kitchen?

"Serve like you're serving a king." That's the same thing I spoke about earlier: feed the hungry, clothe the naked, visit the prisoners – transform lives. The nearest way to a man's heart is in the kitchen. That's how our wives keep us – they learn to feed us. When you can do that you keep a happy person.

If there were one thing you wished everyone would know about those experiencing homelessness, what would that be?

A homeless Vietnam veteran, Larry Mason found a new life through The Bowery Mission.

Fanny Crosby, when she used to speak in the chapel, would say to the men: "You don't have to tell a man he's a sinner – he knows that already." So what we gotta try to do is *live out* the example of Christ as we walk from day to day. Live out that example. It's hard to do sometimes, but we've got to learn to do it if we want to make it into the kingdom.

Any final thoughts?

Remember this: Never look down on a human being, whether it's a man, woman, or child, unless you're trying to pick them up. And all the days of your life you will be blessed. ➤

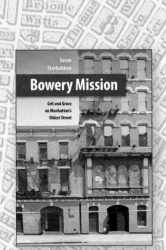

Up Hill

ADRIANO CIRINO

*The story of a
Medellín neighborhood
and its escalators*

Translated by Rahul Bery

ONCE IT WAS CONTROLLED by armed groups on the fringes of the law. Then it was besieged by the army in the largest urban military operation in the history of Colombia. Today, Las Independencias, a neighborhood of fourteen thousand inhabitants in Comuna 13, the "thirteenth commune" of the city of Medellín, is a kind of open-air graffiti art gallery, accessed via a system of outdoor escalators – the only ones ever built in a slum.

Graffiti artists are respected figures in the neighborhood. John Alexander Serna, known as "Chota," is a local celebrity. On a February morning, he emerges from inside Graffilandia, the café-gallery constructed underneath his house, between the third and fourth flights of the escalator system. He's immediately accosted in front of his mural *Operación Orión* by one of the local guides accompanying a group of tourists on a "graffitour" through the neighborhood.

During the 1990s, Medellín was known as the murder capital of the world.

"We're lucky today!" the guide announces. "Chota is one of the most influential artists of Comuna 13."

The gringos ask him for selfies. He obliges for a few moments, then hurries through the crowd toward the escalators, heading down the steep slope. At the bottom, another group of tourists is waiting to watch him do a live painting.

"My work used to go unnoticed," he says. "Now, with the escalators, we're starting to be recognized. They guarantee access to the neighborhood and allow people from around here to display their work to the foreign visitors."

THE FIRST THING YOU SEE in Chota's mural is a woman's face. She is shedding a tear; green shoots grow from it.

By her side, a hand throws a pair of dice onto a bunch of houses typical of the neighborhood. The first die reads "Com. 13"; the second, "16.10.2002."

On October 16, 2002, the then-president of Colombia, Álvaro Uribe, ordered the national army to seize Comuna 13 at the request of Medellín's mayor: a violent intervention decades in the making.

The geographically unpromising area, a very steep hill cut off from the rest of the city, saw a growing number of informal settlements constructed at the end of the 1970s. The area had no utilities and, without official status, the police left it alone. Over the next forty years, the population grew to more than one hundred and thirty thousand people. Throughout the 80s and early 90s, Comuna 13 was contested territory, primarily controlled by Pablo Escobar's cocaine cartel, and by far-right paramilitary groups such as Death to Kidnappers (MAS). The history of the district is a bewildering tangle of alliances and antagonisms; MAS was established to protect members of the cartel and local landowners from the Marxist insurgent groups that kidnapped landowners for ransom and redistributed their land to peasants.

After Escobar's death, the balance of power tipped in favor of the insurgents – the National Liberation Army (ELN), the Revolutionary Armed Forces of Colombia (FARC), the People's Armed Command (CAP). By the turn of the millennium, it had been a generation since the state meaningfully governed the area.

The guerrillas and gangs fought continuously – over the people, over the land, and over San Juan Avenue. Running through Comuna 13, the road is the city's access to the Caribbean coast and the smuggling that a port makes possible. Control of the Comuna is crucial to control of the drug trade.

During this period, the community lived (and died) with shootouts and stray bullets, assassinations and bombings, disappearances and extortion, and the recruitment of minors to serve as foot soldiers in these ongoing wars. During the 1990s, Medellín was known as the murder capital of the world. The violence came to a head in 2000, when right-wing paramilitary groups from the United Self-Defense Forces of Colombia (AUC) also entered the dispute. The levels of crossfire were unprecedented. The killing was most concentrated in Comuna 13, with 357 homicides per 100,000 people by 2002.

And then the state launched Operation Orion. The effort involved nearly fifteen hundred uniformed men: members of the National Army's Fourth Brigade, the Metropolitan Police, and the Special Antiterrorist Forces, as well as other bodies. Their objective: to wipe the ELN, FARC, and CAP militias off the map. The huge public force surrounded the hill and, in a coordinated action with the AUC paramilitaries, attacked at dawn. The battle lasted forty hours and ranged over six neighborhoods, including Las Independencias. Official statistics count just a few deaths, but the National Center for Historical Memory, a public body established by law in 2011, estimates that more than seventy people were killed and three hundred disappeared. There is no doubt that the government forces carried out a number of human rights violations during Operation Orion: torture, illegal detention, kidnapping.

Victims of the conflict are still looking for truth and justice for the abuses committed

Operación Orión was painted by Comuna 13's most prolific artist, John Alexander Serna, also know as Chota.

Adriano Cirino is a journalist at the Federal University of Minas Gerais and the author of Nos bastidores de "Escobar" & outras crônicas bogotanas *(Crivo Editorial, 2018).*

Afternoon popsicles with the guys

by the state. Operation Orion still divides opinion: the militias were eliminated and Comuna 13 was recovered, but at what cost? Some believe that the ends did not justify the means. Others see the operation as a bitter but necessary pill, a last resort that ultimately liberated the community. What is not in dispute is the pivotal nature of those two days. In Comuna 13, there is a time before Operation Orion, and a time after Operation Orion.

WHILE CHOTA DOES HIS PAINTING for the tourists at the base of the hill, up at the top, where the final escalator flight connects with the Media Ladera Viaduct (a walkway) and Balcón de la 13 (a viewing point), another group applauds a performance by a group of young break-dancers. Farther along, a vendor is hawking

souvenirs: "I've got T-shirts, caps, different styles, come take a look!"

It's Víctor Mosquera, a businessman, rapper, and graffiti artist born and raised, like Chota, in Las Independencias. Two years ago he set up a stall on the viaduct, selling tropical fruit to the ever-increasing number of tourists. His stock has changed since then: "All of the T-shirts are personalized," he boasts. "I design them." He's one of Operation Orion's victims, hit by a stray bullet when he was fifteen. He recalls hours of torment, hidden under a bed with his family, waiting for the shooting to stop, the bullet lodged in his arm, until he was able to leave the house and get to a hospital.

"That war pushed us to write, paint, and sing our story," he says. "And that bullet made me grip on to life much harder."

THE GUERRILLAS WERE DRIVEN OUT – but for two more years, the right-wing paramilitaries that had helped the government carry out Operation Orion were the effective government in Comuna 13, judging and executing or "disappearing" those they deemed their enemies. In 2003, these groups surrendered, negotiating amnesty agreements; since then, the state has been in charge.

That's the official version, though there is evidence that a paramilitary-criminal hybrid group run by Escobar's successor, Don Berna, had a lockdown on the city for years afterward. The gangs are still a very significant presence, and in 2011 and 2012, in a bid to maintain power, gangs murdered a dozen Comuna 13 rappers who had spoken out against them. Still, the level of violence has dropped drastically: homicide levels in Medellín as a whole fell 80 percent between 1991 and 2014. The

city finally started investing in the area, to repay what Sergio Fajardo, mayor from 2004 to 2007, called the city's "historical debt" to the poor of Comuna 13, owed after years of abandonment. Fajardo's term saw the implementation of a series of new urban development projects.

The pilot projects were based in Comunas 1 and 2. Their purpose was to build infrastructure, guided by the principles of "social urbanism," the idea that city investment in the most cut-off and chaotic neighborhoods should seek to integrate them with the rest of the city, providing access to the city center along with better lighting and other benefits.

Completed in 2007, the projects

> "That war pushed us to write, paint, and sing our story. And that bullet made me grip on to life much harder."
>
> *Víctor Mosquera*

for Comunas 1 and 2 included widening and improving roads, constructing public schools and parks, and installing a cable car. In 2006 César Augusto Hernández, a civil engineer who was then managing director of the projects, took charge of the Comuna 13 initiative and made his first visits to the community.

Many he spoke to agreed on the immediate problem: the trash. Lacking a reliable system of garbage disposal, it had piled up everywhere. Hernández had an elaborate plan involving pulleys, toboggans, and ducts to transport it to the bottom. "Once a system for trash had been designed," one of the company's documents states, "we also had the idea of designing something so that people could go up and down" the side of the hill.

Many of Comuna 13's inhabitants were limited to local streets, unable to tackle the

The steep hillside on which Comuna 13 sits is now accessible by a system of escalators.

area's steep slopes. Particularly affected were pregnant women, elderly people, and anyone else with compromised mobility, but even the fit and young were hard-pressed to make the scramble up through the tumble of houses on the hillside a part of their daily routine. Residents were also segregated from the rest of the city, cut off from its job opportunities and public services. Those who lived at the top of the hill with jobs in the city center had to hike the equivalent of twenty-eight stories up poorly maintained stairs at the end of each day.

Facing this scenario, Hernández came up with a seemingly ridiculous idea: Why not install escalators on the hillside?

In 2008, the incoming mayor, Alonso Salazar, allowed himself to be persuaded by the engineer's arguments. "I showed him a map of the city," Hernández recalled in an interview, "and the outlines of the escalators that would liberate the ghettos. I told him any mayor could build schools, hospitals, or parks, but that he could do something completely new: reconstruct the social fabric . . . give the community a project that would make them feel something they might never have felt before: pride."

THE MAYOR OPENED BIDS for the escalators' installation in 2010. Accompanied by community leaders, teams of topographers, civil engineers, and architects ventured into the area on trips to assess the situation, and they came up with a plan: the system would be installed in Las Independencias, and would connect to other infrastructure – the Carrera 109 Urban Walkway, the Reversadero, Balcón de la 13, and the Media Ladera Viaduct. Together, these would form a circuit of access for the inhabitants.

"More than anything, the project was about mobility," the architect Juan Carlos Ayure explains. "No one ever thought it would become a tourism thing." He had worked for a private construction company contracted to help remodel the landscape and install the escalators. But before construction began, there was the question of community buy-in. More than thirty houses would have to be purchased and demolished to clear the way.

The city carried out an educational campaign: a series of huge meetings and local assemblies, designed to make residents aware of the benefits and potential risks of the new technology. Many of the neighborhood's inhabitants were so cut off they did not even know what an escalator was.

"How could we explain to these people – people who have few resources, no luxuries, people from a very low social stratum – that there are such things as electric staircases; how do we convince them to let us install them?" asks Ayure. "We took them to places like shopping centers, to show them that there was no need to be scared, that the escalators would not eat them, or swallow them up, that they wouldn't fall." These campaigns were rooted in the ethos of the city's social urbanism, which encourages citizen participation at every stage of the work.

The four-million-dollar project began in February 2011. Nearly three hundred workers were hired, the vast majority of them local. The main qualification was having no criminal background. "We went up there to begin hiring, and it was complete madness," Ayure recalls. "The local hoodlums fought, and there were shootouts during the day" – the slang is "piñata." "People would call me – 'Boss, we've got a piñata!' We had to get a siren. We told the workers: 'Listen guys, when you hear the siren, throw everything onto the floor and run home.'"

Amid these interruptions, the crew widened and paved walkways, repositioned aqueducts and sewage systems, shifted electrical networks, constructed two new public buildings, created green areas, and raised containment walls. Then, at last, came the installation of the escalators.

One of the more Herculean challenges involved transporting the system up the hill: six double flights of escalators, each between eight and fourteen tons. And then there were more subtle difficulties: "We came here with a preliminary final design," says Ayure, "but in a slum like this, a new shack or a new alleyway pops up every week. So my work consisted in finding solutions, once the work was already underway, for all these questions that look so pretty on paper but which in real life are something else entirely."

> **Many of the neighborhood's inhabitants were so cut off they did not even know what an escalator was.**

On December 25, 2011, ten months after the work began, the citizens of Las Independencias inaugurated their escalators. Simultaneously, the city invited neighborhood artists to do graffiti on the façades of nearby houses. The atmosphere was celebratory, and not only because it was Christmas. In a real way, these escalators set the citizens free.

MEDELLÍN WAS NAMED "the most innovative city in the world" in 2013, in a contest promoted by Citigroup, the *Wall Street Journal*, and the Urban Land Institute. Since then, tourism has exploded. Visitors come from all over the world, now drawn to something beyond the narco-tourism and sex tourism that still persist. The new attraction is Comuna 13, and the transformative possibilities of social

Three artists collaborated to create this Comuna 13 mural.

urbanism. According to government data, the Comuna 13 escalators received approximately one hundred and seventy thousand tourists in 2018, 70 percent of them foreigners. And the trend is upward: January 2019 saw close to forty thousand visitors.

This has, of course, changed the neighborhood. The universal problem of gentrification exists here too: while some residents are celebrating the increased value of their homes, others complain about the hike in prices and the cost of living.

Today Las Independencias is a community in which the local and the cosmopolitan cut across each other, collide, and fuse. Consider the foreign lingo that lends names to local attractions, artistic groups, and establishments: Graffitour, Black & White, Coffee Shop Com. 13.

In this neighborhood, walls once studded with bullets are transformed by artists' hands into illuminated manuscripts: the pages of their own recent history, aglow with beauty and memory. The houses, in their turn, shelter a greater and greater variety of businesses – barber shops, grocery stores, clothing and souvenir shops, bars, and galleries.

The escalator system runs for sixteen hours daily, and is operated by a public company. On a February morning, between the second and third flights, Juan Carlos Zapata Holguín, clad in a yellow jumpsuit and black wellingtons, is clasping a pressure cleaner. "Today we're cleaning the escalators and the communal zones," he says. He's one of the fifteen "educational managers," the operators of the escalators who keep them clean and running.

A breakdancer performs on the sidewalk.

He works carefully, occasionally interrupting the stream of water to let people past as they go up and down in a ceaseless flow.

At one point, he darts to the end of the second flight and keeps a woman from tripping. "They look harmless, but these stairs are dangerous," he says. His primary job is to ensure the safety of the users, and to assist those who need it.

The tourists, too, are themselves a kind of hazard. The lack of privacy can be annoying: "Tourists come up to take photos; the view's blocked by the residents' clothes hanging to dry!" Holguín observes. "Or locals go out in the morning wearing pajamas to buy bread for breakfast, and it's embarrassing . . . because suddenly there's a tourist taking photos. . . . They complain, but they like it: business is good."

His colleague, David Andres Zapata, grew up when the neighborhood was under the rule of the guerrillas and the paramilitaries, and witnessed Operation Orion as a child. Before getting the job looking out for the maintenance and safety of the escalators, he helped to install them. For him, the changes that the escalators have brought have been positive. He does not feel invaded, despite the large numbers of tourists: "For many communities, this would be stressful: 'Why can't I walk through my neighborhood?' they would think. But," he claims, "not in Las Independencias. Not here."

Through their art, through the stories they tell each other and those who visit, the pain of their history is transformed into a sense of place. The citizens of Comuna 13 know what they have suffered, they know what they have survived, and they know who they are. ➤

Jane Jacobs's *The Death and Life of Great American Cities* (Random House, 1961) is a classic work of twentieth-century urbanism, its publication a gauntlet thrown down against all the received wisdom of urban planning of its day. And its author was unlikely: a Manhattan housewife and journalist, whose training in urbanism came primarily from her careful observation of how cities actually work, at the close-grain level of the sidewalk.

A good city is made up of good neighborhoods, she wrote, where the mixed use of housing and shopping and other kinds of business ensure a steady flow of human interactions throughout the day. What makes a city safe is what makes it interesting: the presence of people going about their affairs, weaving "a web of public respect and trust."

The charm of the book is its intensely anecdotal nature. Jacobs describes the life of the West Village, and you're drawn into it; this is a book about cities written by someone who loves her own with a fierce realism. Hovering behind the book is the history of her epic struggle with Robert Moses, the high modernist urban planner who, until she challenged him, was well on his way to disfiguring all of New York with his housing projects and highways. *(See reading on page 66.)*

The polis, said Aristotle, "comes into existence, originating in the bare needs of life, and continues in existence for the sake of the good life." In *Till We Have Built Jerusalem* (ISI Books, 2006), Philip Bess dares to take "polis" here to mean simply "city," and he asks this question: What if everything that Aristotle and Thomas Aquinas said about

cities was actually true, and what if we built cities in accordance with that reality?

Bess teaches urban design and architecture at Notre Dame and is active in the New Urbanist movement. He is also a practicing Catholic steeped in the political tradition of the Church.

It's a maddening book – a series of essays which, like the Blake poem that is the origin of its title, can only be called visionary. One of the most outrageous (and probably correct) suggestions he makes is that the canons of urban design implied by Jane Jacobs and developed by the Charter of the New Urbanism aren't just matters of aesthetic preference, but are actually part of the natural law. If what we are called to do is to promote human flourishing, and if brutalist architecture, suburban sprawl, and housing projects don't do that, then they're not just bad – they're wrong. Le Corbusier shouldn't just retire: he should repent.

"The architecture of the third millennium," Bess writes, should "serve the primary symbolic purpose it served in earlier eras – the representation, in orderly, durable, functional, and beautiful buildings, of institutions that enable and encourage us to live as civilized human beings." And the civilized human being is, for Bess, what he is for Saint Thomas: one whose nature, as he lives, with his fellows, in a city with a cathedral at its center, is being drawn to its own perfection and final end, in God.

In a sweaty summer three years after the end of World War II, E. B. White wrote an essay that remains the greatest love letter New York City has ever received. "Here Is New York" (*Holiday Magazine*, 1948) is an attempt to grapple with a very big city in a very small space.

White has a sense of the fragility of New York: the infrastructure that is always overloaded; the systems, so many of them ad hoc, that keep everybody fed; the water of the harbor that always might overrun the seawall. And he has a sense of New York as a target that feels very contemporary: the possibility of nuclear war looms over the end of the essay. Above all, though, he shares with Jacobs the love of the city, because of its meaning as a site of human ambition and collaboration and unlikely fellowship. He writes: "The city is like poetry: It compresses all life, all races and breeds, into a small island and adds music. . . . The island of Manhattan is without any doubt the greatest human concentrate on earth, the poem whose magic is comprehensible to millions . . . but whose full meaning will always remain illusive."

What White did for New York in compressed form, Frederic Morton did for his native Vienna. *Thunder at Twilight: Vienna 1913/1914* (Scribner, 1989) is a cultural history of two years in the life of the city, and if White sees New York as potentially fragile, Morton knows for certain the fragility of Vienna. Those two years – a decade before Morton was born – saw the final flowering of the opulent capital city of the Hapsburg Empire, and the sheer number of people and events concentrated in that one time and place is dazzling. Carnival, 1913: Stalin arrives in Vienna on a mission for those who would become the revolutionaries of 1917. Over the next two years, Hitler paints and rants in beer cellars; Wittgenstein and Freud are each at the center of a separate intellectual circle; the white Lipizzaner stallions perform their highly choreographed dances in the Spanish riding school in the center of the city; everyone is highly strung, there are all the waltzes you

could ask for, and everything seems to point to an explosion. That explosion happens, of course, when the young, potentially liberalizing heir to the throne, the Archduke Franz Ferdinand, is killed with his wife, Sophie, by the Serbian nationalist Gavrilo Princip. Morton's Vienna did not survive World War I, but in his book, its richness lives on.

In 1881, a doctor who had served in the war in Afghanistan has found that his Army pension can't support the cost of the hotel in the Strand where he's been living. He faces a desperate choice: either leave London, or find a housemate. The first option is not to be thought of, and so it's good for him – and for us – that Dr. John Watson meets Sherlock Holmes, who's looking for someone to split the rent at 221B Baker Street.

Arthur Conan Doyle set both *A Study in Scarlet* (1887) and *The Sign of the Four* (1890) in London; of the dozen stories in *The Adventures of Sherlock Holmes* (1892), the first of the collections, all but four take place there. The intense, address-level specificity of the stories gives them a documentary quality: it always seems that Holmes's skill as a detective can't really be separated from his street-by-street knowledge of London itself.

It's Holmes who convinced the world that the city would be the suitable setting for this new genre: something like a thriller, something like an Arthurian quest to bring justice to the land. It's a genre that brings together the romance of the gothic and the chivalry of the legends with the grit and irony of the modern world. Philip Marlowe's Los Angeles and Sam Spade's San Francisco owe Holmes's London a debt, and so, too, does Batman's Gotham City. But Holmes's London still holds the honor of primacy. ⤳

Beneath the Tree of Life

The City of the Age to Come

N. T. WRIGHT

THE GREAT VISION of the New Jerusalem at the end of the Book of Revelation is a vision of ultimate beauty (Rev. 21–22). The word *beauty* doesn't occur much in the Bible, but the celebration of creation all the way from Genesis, through the Psalms and prophets, on into the Gospels and here in Revelation, should alert us to the fact that, though the ancient Jewish people did not theorize about beauty like the Greeks did (that's another story, and a fascinating one, though not for today),

they knew a great deal about it and poured their rich aesthetic sensibility not only into poetry but also into one building in particular: the temple in Jerusalem, whose legendary beauty inspired poets, musicians, and dancers alike. This is the temple where YHWH's glory is glimpsed, not as a retreat *from* the world but as a foretaste of what is promised *for* the whole world. In the great vision of John, the temple has disappeared because the whole city has become a temple; the point of the city is not that it is a place of retreat

Tree of Life at Sunset, sculpture by Kester, Hilario Nhatugueja, Fiel dos Santos, and Adelino Serafim Maté

N. T. Wright, author and New Testament scholar, is the former bishop of Durham in the Church of England. This reading is taken from his book Surprised by Scripture.

from a wicked world but that its new life is poured out into the whole world, to refresh and heal it. . . .

In passages like this we see, with the eye of the apocalyptic visionary, the astonishingly powerful beauty of God's new creation, beauty that should serve as an inspiration to artists and, through their work, to all of us as we seek to give birth to the life of the new creation within the old. The golden city, perfectly proportioned, equal in length and breadth and even, remarkably, height, has, says John, the glory of God and a radiance like a very rare jewel, like jasper, clear as crystal. The wall is built of jasper, while the city itself is pure gold, clear as glass. The foundations are adorned with jewels: jasper, sapphire, agate, emerald, onyx, cornelian, chrysolite, beryl, topaz, chrysoprase, jacinth, and amethyst. The twelve gates are twelve pearls, while the streets of the city are pure gold, transparent as glass. I confess that my knowledge of jewelry is so poor that I can't at once envisage those shining foundations, but I know that whoever wrote this passage delighted in them and wanted readers to do the same, relishing them one by one and in their glittering combination.

I know too that the idea of city streets paved with gold had nothing to do with fabulous wealth – pity the poor human race, when dazzling beauty is reduced to purely monetary function! – but rather with the most ravishing and wonderful beauty imaginable. This is the apocalyptic vision of the beauty of God. And it is given to us not so that in desiring to belong to that city we forget the present world and our obligations within it, but so that we will work to bring glimpses of that glory into the present world, in the peacemaking that anticipates the Isaianic vision of the wolf, the lamb, and the vegetarian lion; in the doing of justice that anticipates the final rule of the true Messiah; in the work of healing that springs from the water of life flowing from the city into the world around; and not least in the glorious art that gives birth to genuine beauty within a world full of ugliness, which bridges the gap between Isaiah's present and future visions, a world full of glory and a world to be filled yet more completely.

In the great vision of John, the temple has disappeared because the whole city has become a temple.

As an aid to this reflection, and to the vocations that follow from it, let me close with a truly remarkable example of the sort of thing I mean. In Revelation 22, the river of life flows from the city to irrigate the surrounding countryside, and on its banks grows the tree of life: not a single tree, as in Genesis, but many trees, now freely available, bearing fruit each month and with leaves for healing. This image of the tree of life and the radical and beautiful healing it promises has generated an extraordinary work of art, commissioned jointly by the British Museum and Christian Aid, and created by artists in Mozambique after the end of that country's long and bitter civil war.

The work is a sculpture of the tree of life. It stands nine or ten feet tall, with branches spreading nine or ten feet in all directions. In it and under its shade are birds and animals. And the whole thing – tree, creatures, and all – is made entirely from decommissioned weapons: bits and pieces of old AK-47s, bullets and machetes and all the horrible paraphernalia of war, most of them made in peaceful Western countries and exported to Mozambique so that the government aid given by the West to that poor country would flow back to our own industries. The point – and it is a stunningly beautiful object at several levels – is that this particular "Tree of Life" reflects the Isaianic promise that swords will be beaten into plow-shares and spears into pruning hooks. The tree stands as a reminder both of the horror of the world, with its multiple human follies and trag-edies, and of the hope of new creation. It has an immediate and powerful message for the people of Mozambique, who had forgotten how to hope, had forgotten that there might be such a thing as peace, as they are invited to sit under the tree and enjoy its fruit and its healing. But it is also a sign of what genuine art can be, taking a symbol from the original creation, building into it full recognition of horrors of the present world that by themselves would lead us to despair, and celebrating the promise for the new world, a world filled with God's glory as the waters cover the sea. It offers celebration without naïveté, sorrow without cynicism, and hope without sentimentality. Standing before it is like glimpsing an apocalyptic vision, a vision of the beauty of God.

Reflecting on this vision ought to inform and direct our thinking and action in many fields of inquiry and endeavor. But for the moment we might do well simply to pause in contemplation and gratitude. This is the vision of God's new heavens and new earth; within that vision, each of us has a particular calling – prophetic, artistic, political, theo-logical, scientific, whatever it may be – by which God will call us to bring signs of that new world to birth within the old one, where vision is still limited and widows still weep. ➤

Source: *Surprised by Scripture* (New York: HarperOne, 2014). Used by permission of the publisher.

Tree of Life, sculpture made of machine gun parts, detail

"And there came unto me one of the seven angels . . . and talked with me, saying, Come hither, I will shew thee the bride, the Lamb's wife. And he carried me away in the spirit to a great and high mountain, and shewed me that great city, the holy Jerusalem, descending out of heaven from God, having the glory of God: and her light was like unto a stone most precious, even like a jasper stone, clear as crystal."

Revelation 21:9–11

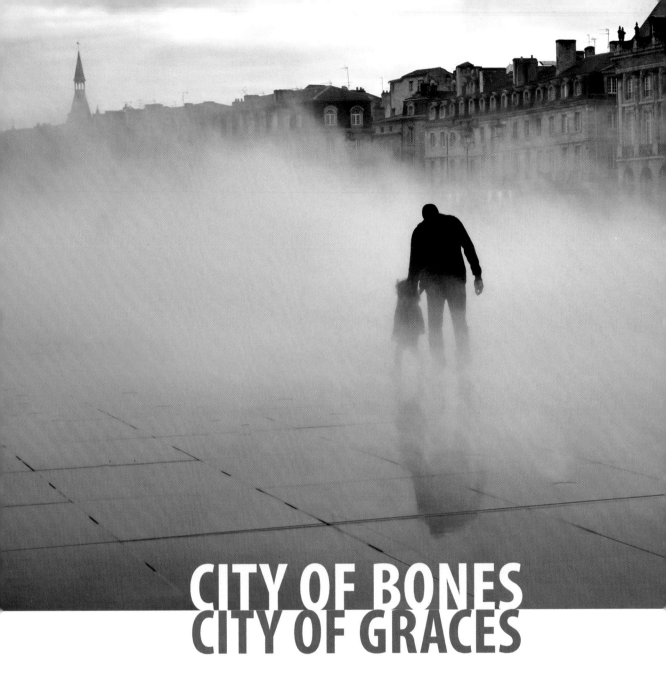

CITY OF BONES CITY OF GRACES

JOSEPH BOTTUM

Valentino Belloni, *Father and Daughter*

THE CITY STINKS. This city, that city, every city everywhere: They reek of sour urine, old vomit, rotting food, the slow tidal surge of human excrement down in the sewers.

Want an image of the metropolis? A depiction of the thing in itself? Think of a night scene, like a cityscape in a photorealist painting, where a thin, scabrous rat scrabbles up from a storm drain to gnaw at a dead pigeon in the gutter. The abandoned warehouses, the smog-stained brick, make a dark canyon of the street, and trash skitters along the filthy sidewalk. High above, an illuminated billboard advertises diamonds, as worn by an elegant, near-orgasmic woman in a blue dress. Another brightly lit sign urges passersby – in a clumsy, overexcited red font – to call a shyster lawyer and sue someone. There's even a picture of the lawyer on the sign. He wears a yellow tie and smirks.

London, Los Angeles, Lahore: the place hardly matters. All urban spaces have that deep ineradicable stench of so many people so close together. They all decay. They foster the commerce of dishonesty. They breed disease. Peel back the centuries of cracked pavements. The subways, sewers, and rusted steam pipes. The stained soil crushed beneath the city's unnatural weight. And even then we would not discover the enchanted whisper of beginning, the fresh green breast of a new world. Peel back the city to the time of its foundation. Peel back the corpses piled on corpses, the generations of violence. Peel it back to the bare ground of origin, and all we would find is the first grave of a founding murder. The city is built on death, all the way down. A city of bones.

THERE'S ANOTHER CITY, too, of course. Or, at least, another way to see it: The city is the place of flowers, cut carnations and roses in buckets at the corner grocery. The city is the place of parks and tree-lined boulevards and flags waving over paved streets. The place of awnings and marble vestibules. The place of manners, for that matter: No civilization exists without the *civitas*. No urbanity without the urban. Nothing politic without the polis.

Want a counter image of a metropolitan world? Imagine, maybe, breakfasting on croissants and café au lait, "Early in the morning / Of a lovely summer day," to quote the poet Robert Hillyer:

They were hosing the hot pavement
With a dash of flashing spray
And a smell of summer showers
When the dust is drenched away,
Under greenery like scenery,
Rue François Premier.

Or imagine being in a cityscape painting. Strolling, say, under an umbrella in Gustave Caillebotte's *Paris Street, Rainy Day*. Or something in a softer focus, like Claude Monet's *Houses of Parliament, Sunset*. For that matter, something harder edged, like Marc Chagall's *Paris through the Window*.

The city is home to museums, symphonies, ballet, and opera – all the civilized arts that exist only thanks to public munificence. The virtue of generosity proves difficult for the rich: acts of charity are generous only when they come with sacrifice, and the truly wealthy sacrifice little even when they give much. But Aristotle gives us another name for the good act of making grand gifts. He calls it the virtue of munificence: donations to public life so large that only the wealthy can undertake them. And the city is the place where munificence can flower.

The great cities are neither vile stinkpots nor enchanted gardens.

The place of bustle and beauty. The location of charity and civilization. A land of fountains. The home for vast swaths of the laughter and joy of human interaction. The city is the woman leaning against the man on the park bench on a summer's weekend morning. The city is the Salvation Army Santa who rings his bell and laughs as the Christmas snow flitters down. The city is the people streaming by who smile and push a dollar bill into his red kettle. The city is

---

Joseph Bottum is director of the Classics Institute at Dakota State University.

the schoolgirl in the navy-blue tam who ducks behind a tree to hide from her dog, then relents and darts out to scoop the anxious dachshund up into a hug. A city of small graces.

OF COURSE, NO ONE HAS ever truly lived in either of these, the City of Bones or the City of Graces. We experience only some strange amalgam of them both: corruption and decency, malice and benevolence, side by side. The great cities are neither vile stinkpots nor enchanted gardens. Not completely. They are only beautiful failures and corrupt successes.

Even the city besieged by warfare has its redeeming virtues. Even the most glittering utopia has its hidden sins.

> **Wicked Sodom and Gomorrah seem to manifest the deep truth about cities – until, suddenly, they don't.**

Where does the city come from? Economics is often invoked to explain the birth of cities in ancient times, and fair enough: the city has proved to be the greatest economic engine the world has ever known. But when human beings first gave up nomadic life, it was not because they understood the financial advantages of collected reservoirs of capital and the monetary effects of the division of labor. Even the word *economics* shows its late origin: Derived from *oikonomia*, the ancient Greek word for managing a household, economics became a term for the king's budget, the management of the royal household, and thereby grew in late medieval times to mean the financial management of the nation.

In *The Ancient City* (1864), the historian Fustel de Coulanges makes the case that the birth of the city is literally from the grave. Coulanges argues that nomadic peoples tended to bury their dead in particular spots. And that gradually led to temples near the tombs, then marketplaces near the temples, then houses near the marketplaces.

Then of course there is political theory, civilization as refuge from Thomas Hobbes's nasty, brutish state of nature. In anthropology, René Girard points out that mythology almost always places death at the birth of civilization. Perhaps the city was born from fear about our own deaths. Or perhaps the city was born from grief at the death of others. Either way, the city begins with death.

IN THE BIBLE, the first city is founded by Cain, the first murderer. From there on, Scripture radiates a steady mistrust of cities – a constant sense that cities are defined by the temptations they offer, the occasions they provide for sin. Prophets come from the desert and the pastures; corruption comes from the city. Even in the Holy Land, the Ark of the Covenant rests in the country camp of Shiloh, rather than in the conquered cities. Wicked Sodom and Gomorrah seem to manifest the deep truth about cities – until, suddenly, they don't. The Psalms, and then the prophets after David, offer a different vision of the city. Its name is Jerusalem.

This is how Saint Augustine reads civic history in *The City of God*. "Cain (signifying 'possession'), the founder of the earthly city, and his son Enoch (meaning 'dedication'), in whose name it was founded, indicate that this city is earthly both in its beginning and in its end – a city in which nothing more is hoped for than can be seen in this world." Augustine points out how Genesis specifies the professions of the line of Cain: six generations on, there is Jabal, "the father of such as dwell in tents, and of such as have cattle"; Jubal, "the father of all such as handle the harp and

Valentino
Belloni,
Crunched

organ"; Tubal-Cain, "an instructor of every artificer in brass and iron"; and Naamah, whose name means *beauty* or *pleasure*.

These brothers are described as founding the skills necessary for city life, and their sister helps establish the temptations of the city – including (according to rabbinical interpretations) her beautiful songs for worshiping idols. What follows is the brief poem, the "Song of the Sword," that their father, Lamech, sings:

Hear my voice; ye wives of Lamech,
hearken unto my speech:
for I have slain a man to my wounding,
and a young man to my hurt.
If Cain shall be avenged sevenfold,
truly Lamech seventy and sevenfold.
(Gen. 4:23–24)

The origin in violence was signaled when Cain established the first city, and the continuing violence was declared in Lamech's "Song of the Sword." The City of Bones is built on murder, all the way down.

But then David brings the Ark into Jerusalem, and the Bible begins to tell a counter story. Before David, the Bible contrasted the sinful violence of the city with the peace of Eden, the idyllic world of innocence in the garden. After David, the Bible tends to contrast the violence and corruption of the actual city – such as Babylon and Nineveh – with the peace of the ideal city.

Isaiah famously promises that when God judges among the nations, the people of earth "shall beat their swords into plowshares, and their spears into pruning hooks: nation shall not lift up sword against nation, neither shall they learn war anymore" (Isa. 2:2–4). But that prophecy comes immediately after the assurance that "out of Zion shall go forth the law, and the word of the Lord from Jerusalem" – a peace that can derive only from a holy city, not a city of death. And even then, it is only promised "in the last days" – an apocalyptic ideal of the city, not its reality even in the actual present city of Jerusalem.

Augustine argues that this is a vision of the City of God, which stands over against the City of Man. We must live in one city: the polis, with its civic structures struggling to constrain the

constant threat of escalating violence. But we are called to the other city: the idea of the New Jerusalem, which develops from the prophesies of Ezekiel through the Book of Revelation.

The Bible begins with a garden and ends with a city, as Jacques Ellul and others after him have noted. In *The Meaning of the City* (1951), Ellul argues that God's plan develops through sacred history along this trajectory. Ellul himself was suspicious of actual cities, seeing urban life as a constraint on human freedom and autonomy. But he recognizes the apocalyptic picture of Revelation as an important departure from other ancient religions: the Bible does not promise a return to idyllic beginnings. In place of the first innocence of the Garden of Eden, we have the second innocence of the New Jerusalem, where "there shall be no more curse" (Rev. 22:3–4). This "great city, the holy Jerusalem, descending out of heaven from God" promises an end to the emotions of death – both anxiety at our own deaths and grief at the deaths of others: "And God shall wipe away all tears from their eyes; and there shall be no more death, neither

sorrow, nor crying, neither shall there be any more pain: for the former things are passed away" (Rev. 21:4–18).

H ow to understand human cities against this prophetic ideal?

Oh, we've pictured the city righteously destroyed, like Sodom and Gomorrah. Nathanael West's 1939 novel about hateful Los Angeles, *The Day of the Locust*, ends with a picture of the city burning: the dry Santa Ana winds pulling out all the moisture from the wooden bungalows till they are nothing but kindling for the great cleansing fire. We've even pictured the city as deserving a destruction that never quite comes, as though God had abandoned even his wrath against us. The billboard, advertising an optometrist, that looms above the valley of ashes in *The Great Gatsby*, for example: "Above the grey land and the spasms of bleak dust which drift endlessly over it, you perceive, after a moment, the eyes of Doctor T. J. Eckleburg."

But in the vision of a city not founded on murder, we may spy a path to redemption for the actual cities in which we dwell. It is precisely our call to the not-yet-come City of God that allows us to work for the bettering of the City of Man. William Blake, taking in the "dark Satanic Mills" of industrial England, imagines the apocalypse restoring nature and holiness to the troubled earth, and commits himself: "I will not cease from Mental Fight, / Nor shall my sword sleep in my hand: / Till we have built Jerusalem, / In England's green & pleasant Land."

Yet even the desire to perfect the earthly city can result in a reenacting of the sin of Cain. An extreme example is the Taiping Rebellion – the bloodiest human conflict outside the world wars – which captured Nanking in 1853, and renamed it "New Jerusalem."

IN NEW YORK, the herds of yellow taxis stampede down Fifth Avenue to Washington Square, on through the switchback ravines of Greenwich Village, and on to the canyons of Wall Street. Across the ocean, similar herds stream through London. Krakow may be all the way around the world from Salvador da Bahia, but in both the Polish royal town and the Brazilian colonial city, you can walk among the old high Catholic buildings – proving that all we need to have block after block of surviving Baroque architecture is a city that was wealthy at the right moment and too poor in later centuries to tear it down and build something new. Even with all their differences, cities mirror other cities' traits and features.

Ankara, Brasília, Versailles, and Las Vegas, for example. Each as different as can be, but they share something strange: a disquieting uniformity in the eras of their architecture, the result of being built all at once. Rome, Ezra Pound once complained, is the only city run like a museum. But every Mediterranean city

sometimes feels that way. Every city on a coast, Albert Camus once pointed out, turns either its back or its face to the sea. Charleston and Miami are American cities with their bright faces to the water. Tacoma and New York are cities that have turned inward, pushing their dark warehouses near the ocean.

I remember sitting once, late at night, in a diner in South San Francisco, reading Ron Hansen's 1996 novel, *Atticus*. The fog pulsed by the windows in waves. The airplanes at the nearby airport roared every few moments. The coffee was the old American standard of percolator-burned pale brown swill. And the novel – ah, yes, the novel. In his Prodigal Son–framed tale of a modern rancher and his missing son, Hansen built an elaborate symbol from a sundog, that odd atmospheric phenomenon in which a small second sun seems to float around 22 degrees off to the left or right of the actual sun. In *Atticus*, the sundog seemed to symbolize the relation of fathers and sons, and the strangeness of the physical world, and maybe even the Eucharist.

Could there be a rich symbol like that for the city?

Down in its inward essence, the city is vile. Up at its true ideal, the city is noble. We've only experienced the mixed middle thing: a little bit cursed, a little bit blessed. An occasion of sin and an opportunity for charity. A stain of ugliness and a flash of beauty.

A human thing, in other words – laden with the guilt of Cain, but straining toward the New Jerusalem. ⤴

> Yet even the desire to perfect the earthly city can result in a reenacting of the sin of Cain.

The Eternal People

PHILIP BRITTS

Forty years after the death of Philip Britts (1917–1949), this poem was discovered among the papers of a friend. Britts was a farmer, poet, activist, and pastor who joined an international pacifist community, the Bruderhof, in the early days of World War II. Soon he, along with the community, was forced to leave Europe for South America, where he contracted a rare fungal disease that led to his death at the age of thirty-one. This poem is taken from *Water at the Roots: Poems and Insights of a Visionary Farmer* (Plough, 2018).

Images in this piece: Rober H. Meltzer, *Taos Pueblo Scene*; Rob Pointon, *Tram Trails*; Bijay Biswaal, *Wet Platform IV*; Beni Gassenbauer, *Enlightenment.*

When a nation sallies against another nation,
With spears or muskets, cannon or tanks,
For a year or for a generation,
That is not the true warfare,
Nor is that the eternal city.

And when one has proved itself the stronger,
And politicians ponder terms of peace,
And armies are recalled, and penalties are paid,
And the normal national life begins again
In pride or in humiliation,
That is not the true peace, the ultimate peace.

The combat ends and slowly is forgotten,
The political peace is sooner or later broken,
And sooner or later the city and the people
  become only a memory.

Is the eternal city full of gilded towers?
Are the streets broad and paved with marble?
Is she defended by gates of steel that endure?
And are her palaces of polished gold?

And the eternal people, are they strong?
Are they comely, are they stately in their walk?
Are they keener of intellect than other men,
And have they greater courage?

No, but the eternal city is other than this, and the eternal people are other than this.

At times the city is a group of plaster cottages,
At times the city is built of wood with roofs of grass,
At times the city is a circle of tents pitched by a river.
At times the city is a clearing in a forest,
    with watch-fires but no houses.

And the eternal people are as other people, no taller, no braver, no stronger, no cleverer.

In the eternal people many are weak,
Many are slow-thinking, many are timid.
The eternal people are as other people,
Only their eyes are more like the eyes of children,
Shining with the freedom of the eternal city.

For the enemy attacks each one in his own heart,
And must be fought continually, each in his own blood.
And the hardness of the fight is that the enemy attacks in disguise,
He comes as a friend or a champion,
And is beautiful or desirable,
But he is a traitor, and his beauty turns to hideousness.
And the problem of the eternal people is to recognize the enemy,
For when he is revealed his power is broken.

The weapons of the eternal people are not carnal weapons,
The weapons of the eternal people are the will to Truth,
The will to unity and the means to unity which is Love
And above all, loyalty to the invisible King.

Part of the eternal city may be in one country,
And part may be a thousand miles away.
It is not a matter of space,
It is a matter of the unity of heart and mind
    against the common enemy.
And the enemy of the eternal people is the Prince of Death.

These are the commands of the invisible King:
That they are not divided against each other,
Either in spiritual pride or in material competition,
But that each sees in the other his comrade in arms,
And has perfect love towards him and helps him in the fight,
And that they be all brothers fighting side by side the eternal warfare.
And the measure of the strength of the eternal people
Is the measure of their obedience to the invisible King.

Small Acts of Grace

Building Urban Community in Pittsburgh

BRANDON McGINLEY

Tony Taj,
The Skyline,
mixed media
on canvas,
2011

THIS STORY BEGINS with an event I considered a flop. It was on March 19, 2016, the Feast of Saint Joseph. The email I had sent to friends around Pittsburgh went like this:

> Please join us for a potluck dinner . . . to discuss ways young Catholics in Pittsburgh can effectively adapt to the challenges of modern, secular(izing) society. Historically Catholics naturally formed communities of support – spiritual, social, financial, etc. – through neighborhoods, parishes, and other associations. How can we form

intentional communities in this day and age that express Catholic uniqueness while still actively engaging in the wider world? How can we help one another more effectively?

The problem with the event was turnout – too much of it. With food and seating and children to be organized, not a great deal of actual conversation happened, and what did was disjointed and unfocused. There was obviously interest in organizing a common life to counter the alienation of secular liberalism, but we hadn't even figured out how to talk about it.

In the nearly four years since that potluck,

some of the invitees have moved to other cities or elsewhere around the city. But several of us have settled in a single neighborhood in south Pittsburgh called Brookline. Without ever really trying, we have brought into reality the abstract notions that were on the table at that chaotic gathering.

No one decided that Brookline was going to host a capital-c Community. We were the second family among our friends to move to the neighborhood, mostly for its housing, walkability, and affordability. That we would be living three blocks from friends was a bonus.

But then a third friend-family chose Brookline, and the house they bought was catty-corner from the first. How convenient! Three families could walk to each other's houses for cookouts or birthdays or a game of cards. As 2016 rolled on, however, we came to realize that there were really seven families, all of whom lived either in south Pittsburgh or nearby suburbs, who were spending a lot of time together.

We had another meeting, just the seven families. This time, we learned our lesson and got a teenager to watch the kids while the parents talked. In our conversation, we recognized that *something* was happening organically: proximity, shared values, and similar-aged children were drawing us to one another. We decided to take action to confirm and develop these friendships, rather than permit them to be worn down by the relentless winds of alienation, dislocation, and anxiety.

We established an online group chat so that we could stay in touch throughout the day to offer or ask for help and prayer, plan events, seek advice, or just vent about the latest toddler atrocity. The point was explicitly to augment and facilitate real-world interactions, never to replace them. And we committed to prioritizing one another with our time and attention, to be willing to give freely and cheerfully without a spirit of calculation and quid pro quo, to treat each other – increasingly as trust grows over time – like family.

From the beginning, I always used the language of "community" to describe this effort. After all, I tend to think in terms of grand and abstract concepts, so my vision was expansive. But these friends consistently tried to reel me in, and after a while I finally got the picture: what we were describing and attempting was not engineering a society, but simply living as genuine friends.

M Y FAMILY WAS on a Virginia highway when our phones pinged. It was a notification from the group chat, and it was urgent: one of our friends' boys desperately needed prayers. There were no details, but it was especially distressing that the message came from someone other than his parents. Whatever had happened, they were apparently too frantic to post it themselves.

We were helpless to support them physically. But we could pray. And so together with our children we prayed as we careened down the dark Virginia byways. And we felt united to our friends, who were also praying in their homes, or maybe on other roads.

The boy, we found out later, had fallen out of a tree and cracked his head on a root. The damage was millimeters from severing an auditory nerve and nicking the carotid artery. But he would be, and is now, fine.

These days, six of our seven families live in Brookline. Remarkably, the seventh family, with a suburban residency requirement due to the father's job, moved across their town to

Brandon McGinley is a writer, editor, and speaker whose work has appeared in publications such as First Things *and the* Catholic Herald. *He lives in Pittsburgh with his wife and four children.*

Brookline families gather on a Pittsburgh sidewalk.

be as close as possible to our neighborhood. No one asked any of the families to move; we had never made a specific commitment to that kind of proximity. But the benefits were apparent, so they accelerated their new-house timelines and transferred their belongings five or ten minutes away.

Brookline was once one of the most dynamic Catholic neighborhoods in a city of Catholic neighborhoods. Its parish, the Church of the Resurrection, was the largest parish with the largest school in the diocese. Now, although Pew hasn't done a study on us, it would be fair to assume that "lapsed Catholic" is the commonest religious identity among our neighbors.

It's tempting to say that we are trying to restore that lost mid-century legacy. And there are times when it feels that way, like when I lean out the window of our minivan to chat with one of our friends' boys on his bike. But friendship isn't about conforming ourselves to some historic model. It's about conforming ourselves to Christ in the circumstances with which God has presented us.

It is inspiring to see other examples of this, even if we share only modestly in their radicalism. My family has twice visited the Bruderhof home in Pittsburgh, where university students from the New Meadow Run and Spring Valley communities live during their studies, and we yearn to visit more often. And

I have been fortunate to have been hosted at the Fox Hill community in the Hudson Valley. Places like these, and the people whose love of Christ and their neighbor give them life and peace, fill us with confidence that Christian community is not only *possible* in these days, but *essential*.

Because the truth is that the old model, whatever its features and bugs, is not available to us. Those old neighborhoods were built on a substrate of Christian culture that has long since eroded – partly as a result of the faithless profligacy of precisely the communities it sustained. Whatever we're doing, and whatever we do moving forward, it must be undertaken with a clear-eyed understanding that we are building nearly from scratch. Our project is not one of reclamation, but of laying the first beams of the scaffolding that will support a rebirth of community-based Christian witness in decades and generations to come.

I HAD A GOLF DATE with a couple of the neighborhood dads. But when I called one of them to confirm, I could tell from his tone that something was wrong. His family was hosting another family's three boys because their mother was experiencing alarming symptoms in her pregnancy. The emergency ultrasound revealed death in the cradle of life.

The mourning parents returned for their other children and cried with their friends. We had them over a few days later, the evening before the mother was delivered of her baby's body. Her husband observed that she had become a living icon of the Pietà. I thought of the embrace we had shared when he first told me of the pregnancy.

The family arranged a funeral for baby Angelus; the parlor and the cemetery provided everything gratis. All the children old enough to wield a trowel tossed earth into the tiny tomb. To share in play is to share in pain. To share in joy is to share in sorrow. To share in life is to share in death.

W E OFTEN THINK of the married couple as the generative unit of Christian community, but that's incomplete. Of course, it is the business of a husband and wife, in cooperation with the Creator, to beget the next generation. Accordingly, in the Christian imagination the household of parents and their children, patterned after the Holy Family, rightly holds a privileged position. But an exclusive focus on the nuclear family runs the risk of reducing the abundant life of which Jesus speaks (John 10:10) to biological fertility. That falls short of the gospel. Within the church, the spiritual fecundity of grace seeds and nurtures God's presence among us, making genuine communion of persons possible in this life.

In other words, friendship is fertile. Not only do proximity and solidarity create the material, social, and spiritual stability that allows for more children to be welcomed with confidence, but relationships of mutual charity also become channels of grace. And because authentic friendship is both spiritual and corporeal, it is also sacramental. In the Catholic Church, the sacraments are said to be "efficacious signs of grace" that bring into being the spiritual realities they signify. While bringing a meal to a postpartum mother or grasping the shoulder of a struggling father or gently correcting another family's child are not numbered among the seven sacraments, they are acts of trust and service that communicate grace.

Taken together, these small acts form a matrix that pulses with divine life. They form the foundation for living together in ways that our secular-individualist culture finds frightening in its vulnerability and impractical in its self-giving.

And yet, confronted with the possibility of genuine community, people become fascinated, captivated, entranced. That's because we humans know that living as isolated individuals or families is not how it's meant to be. Somewhere deep in our souls the words are carved, "It is not good for man to be alone."

It's now becoming clear that the Brookline experiment is overtopping the levees of friendship alone. Several new families have moved to the neighborhood – some looking to take part in our little something, some stumbling into it – and we've integrated a few who were already around. We're hoping to attract people in different stages of life – younger, older, single, childless – but no one really knows how to go about that, except to seize the opportunities God places in front of us.

There's no denying that we're now in the community-building business. To do so would be to frustrate the fecundity of grace; it would be to ignore the lesson we learned a few years ago, when we recognized something was happening and took the initiative to ensure it continued to happen. Community is the organic extension of friendship, but it requires, especially these days, a little light-touch intentionality to catalyze and nurture it.

Those first friendships remain the

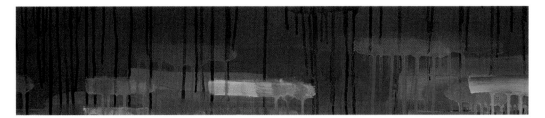

fusion-core that provides energy and gravity to the entire system. But grace proliferates. That means there will be new friendships, new life-giving cores of sacramentality, that will over time form an impossibly complicated Venn diagram of irruptions of heaven.

ONE LATE SUMMER AFTERNOON, several families, including a few new additions, agreed to meet for ice cream at Scoops on the Boulevard. We prayed a rosary as we walked to the main street, and then we clogged the sidewalk with sticky-fingered children until one of the new families suggested we decamp to their home a block away.

We all climbed a Pittsburgh slope – a block here is often more grueling than a mile in Omaha – and gathered on their generous front porch. The kids ran around and around and around while the parents talked and talked and talked, rocking babies and pouring lemonades.

Midsummer dusk approached, and everyone gathered up their protesting children for the walk home. At least one of ours fell asleep on the way.

I make it all sound idyllic, and often it really is. In the moment, of course, one gets preoccupied with child discipline and safety, and the blessings of togetherness can feel a bit abstract. But, nearly without fail, on the way home or in the last moments before sleep we say, "I'm glad we went. It was a good day."

We know there will always be troubles. Little kid mischief becomes big kid mischief. And of course adults can break trust, too. (To respect privacy, I haven't discussed any specific challenges here.) We've been upfront about this among ourselves, committing to the kind of intentional trust-building that will allow us, God willing, to confront serious problems with directness.

For now, though, we feel unduly blessed with peace and good order. For now, and we pray forever, we feel confident that this is sustainable.

Because in truth it is sustainable, because grace is infinitely sustainable.

Fear of the vulnerability of trust is said to be a realistic response to the Christian truth of the Fall and our unavoidable brokenness. But when seemingly prudent caution prevents us from making commitments of mutual self-sacrifice, it becomes despair of the healing power of grace – rendering impossible precisely the solidarity on which friendship, community, and society are founded. The result isn't protecting ourselves from others' potentially toxic brokenness, but wallowing in our own.

If Brookline is to become a fruitful example of Christian community, it will not be as a reproducible template or, God forbid, a celebrated "model community." Rather, it will be as a place where the healing power of grace has simply been allowed to work as it should, where people with radically different personalities, strengths, and weaknesses are able to share life and death secure in our shared identity in Christ.

The episcopal motto of David Zubik, bishop of Pittsburgh, is, "Nothing is impossible for God." I admit that, in comparison with the traditionally grand Latin mottos, I had long felt this one was a bit trite. But now I see its majesty. And maybe, just maybe, Brookline is poised to demonstrate that majesty to this city. ⇒

In the Valley of Lemons

JOSE CORPAS

WHEN TITA EVERTSZ first set foot in La Limonada in 1994, she was walking into one of the most dangerous slums in Guatemala City, a city that then had one of Latin America's highest homicide rates. It was a neighborhood that the police rarely entered, even though it is home to more than sixty thousand people and sits at the foot of the country's Supreme Court building. On that first day, Tita didn't know what she was getting into. But twenty-five years later, she's still there.

Back when my grandmother was young, La Limonada was largely uninhabited, a ravine of foliage about one mile long by half a mile wide, split by a winding stream. She would tell me stories about it on childhood visits to Guatemala – stories of a valley filled with lemon trees. There were so many lemons, she said, that in the early morning or late evening, when the sun was a deep orange and the dew rose to eye level, you could stand on the damp soil of the ravine, open your mouth, and feel drops of lemonade on your tongue.

When I repeated this description to Tita, a delicate woman with a face dominated by her smile, she laughed. The citrus groves are long gone. But today, she said, the name is still

The green-walled Limón Academy was founded by Tita Evertsz in La Limonada, Guatemala City.

Jose Corpas has written two books on boxing history and has been published by ESPN, Narratively, *and the* Acentos Review.

Tita Evertsz

deserved, since the people who live here are "as tough as lemons." She grinned and made a fist.

The once-lush ravine is now crowded with cinderblock shanties, their tin roofs held in place with more cinderblocks or scrap metal. The stream still flows but is chocolate-colored, mixed with trash and sewage redirected from other parts of the city.

The first influx of squatters who settled here used it as a hiding place – an alternative to ending up in a grave. They were refugees from the repression that followed the CIA-backed overthrow in 1954 of Guatemala's President Jacobo Árbenz, a democratically elected leader with socialist leanings. The government-sponsored reign of terror lasted more than three decades and left at least two hundred thousand people dead or disappeared. The ones who escaped to La Limonada built shacks and used rainwater for bathing, cooking, and drinking. Though the number of settlers quickly reached into the thousands, they were considered homeless and did not figure in government census reports. Since then, several generations of neighborhood residents have spent their lives

working menial jobs, hustling, and begging. It's not a place where nuclear families last long; what takes their place is gang life.

Standing at the edge of the La Limonada ravine is like looking down into a crater of stalled dreams – "the cemetery of the living," as journalist José Alejandro Adamuz Hortelano has called it. But Tita Evertsz doesn't see it that way. "I sit at the edge of La Limonada and all I smell is hope."

I N 1994, before she first entered La Limonada, Tita had been volunteering at a nearby general hospital when a mother and her ten-year-old daughter were rushed into the emergency room. Much of their skin had been scorched away; the match that started the blaze had been lit by the woman's husband. Tita spent days at the girl's side. There she had an epiphany: "Rather than fish bodies out at the mouth of the river, I decided it was better to go upstream to see who, or what, was throwing them in."

Without knowing what to expect, Tita walked into the La Limonada ravine. Homes with no windows flanked alleyways only a few feet wide. Low-slung clotheslines of wet T-shirts hung inches above her head.

It was a dark time of her life, Tita told me, but also one that set her on her path. A mother of four, she returned a few days after her first visit, pushing a stroller with her four-year-old daughter and a pot of rice and beans inside. She handed out food to hungry children and single moms. Walking among the neighborhood's gang members, dealers, and addicts, Tita saw something of herself in the faces around her: she had spent years in an abusive relationship and was no stranger to the allure of drugs. She prayed: "Lord, help me to prevent this and not have to heal it."

She soon decided to focus on the children of the neighborhood. Within a year, she founded Vidas Plenas (Full Lives), whose mission, as stated on the organization's website, has been to "support the physical, educational, social, emotional, and spiritual needs of the children, youth, adults, and families of La Limonada and other communities that need it." At first, she met with resistance from some residents, especially the drug dealers, who saw her efforts as a threat to their influence. Then it took her several years to find a suitable location for the school she wanted to start. But she persisted, and in the year 2000, the first students filed through the school doors.

The school is now called Limón Academy, after the neighborhood's signature fruit. Since then, it's been joined by three additional schools (a fourth is under construction) named for the mandarin, orange, and grapefruit. Approximately four hundred children now attend these academies, served by a staff of forty. The schools charge no tuition and receive no government assistance; they seek to supplement the children's public education and serve as community centers. The only requirement for parents is mandatory attendance at a monthly parenting class where they receive counseling and updates on their child's progress. "Focusing only on the children is like trying to fly a plane with one wing," Tita says. "We needed to get the parents – the second wing – involved."

A typical day at the academies starts with the children, aged two to twelve, washing their hands, taking a vitamin, eating a balanced meal, and brushing their teeth. After a short Bible study, they do their homework, study art, or engage in sports and physical education.

The academies can't save everyone, of course. Students regularly drop out, falling victim to necessity or temptation, and even those who stay must contend with the pull of criminal activity. Amelia, for example, comes from a family of thieves, a skill they passed down to her. Stealing is still her family's livelihood – but Amelia says that, thanks to Tita, she "steals less now."

Other students' stories are of outright success. Several alumni have gone on to complete college, taking advantage of scholarships Tita has offered. One former student, Abby, is now a teacher at one of the academies.

If you stand at the rim of the ravine and know where to look, you can spot the brightly colored academies of Limón, Mandarina, Naranja, and Toronja below. You can see roses growing in pots on window sills and freshly washed teddy bears hung out to dry in the warm air. The air doesn't taste like lemonade, but it is full of hope. ➤

> **I sit at the edge of La Limonada and all I smell is hope.**

To learn more, visit lemonadeinternational.org *or* vidasplenas.org.

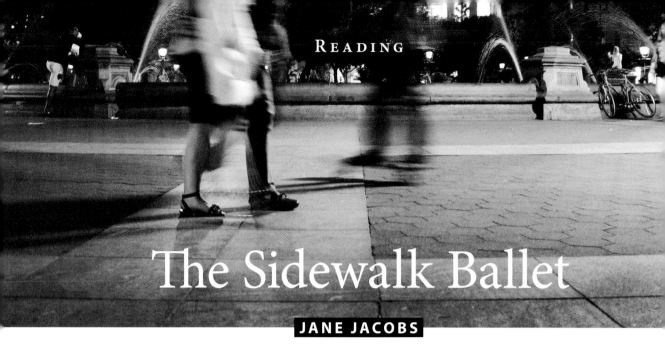

The Sidewalk Ballet

JANE JACOBS

Writer, activist, and pioneer of New Urbanism, Jane Jacobs (1916–2006) fought to save Manhattan's "old city" neighborhoods from being obliterated in urban renewal projects. This reading is from her 1961 classic The Death and Life of Great American Cities.

Phil Roeder, *Nighttime in Greenwich Village*

UNDER THE SEEMING DISORDER OF the old city, wherever the old city is working successfully, is a marvelous order for maintaining the safety of the streets and the freedom of the city. It is a complex order. Its essence is intricacy of sidewalk use, bringing with it a constant succession of eyes. This order is all composed of movement and change, and although it is life, not art, we may fancifully call it the art form of the city and liken it to the dance – not to a simple-minded precision dance with everyone kicking up at the same time, twirling in unison and bowing off en masse, but to an intricate ballet in which the individual dancers and ensembles all have distinctive parts which miraculously reinforce each other and compose an orderly whole.

THE BALLET OF THE GOOD CITY SIDEWALK never repeats itself from place to place, and in any one place is always replete with new improvisations. The stretch of Hudson Street where I live is each day the scene of an intricate sidewalk ballet. I make my own first entrance into it a little after eight when I put out the garbage can, surely a prosaic occupation, but I enjoy my part, my little clang, as the droves of junior high school students walk by the center of the stage dropping candy wrappers. (How do they eat so much candy so early in the morning?) While I sweep up the wrappers I watch the other rituals of morning: Mr. Halpert unlocking the laundry's handcart from its mooring to a cellar door, Joe Cornacchia's son-in-law stacking out the empty crates from the delicatessen, the barber bringing out his sidewalk folding chair, Mr. Goldstein arranging the coils of wire which proclaim the hardware store is open, the wife of the tenement's superintendent depositing her chunky three-year-old with a toy mandolin on the stoop, the vantage point from which he is learning the English his mother cannot speak. Now the primary children, heading for

St. Luke's, dribble through to the south; the children for St. Veronica's cross, heading to the west, and the children for P.S. 41, heading toward the east. . . .

THE HEART-OF-THE-DAY BALLET I SELDOM SEE, because part of the nature of it is that working people who live there, like me, are mostly gone, filling the roles of strangers on other sidewalks. But from days off, I know enough of it to know that it becomes more and more intricate.

LONGSHOREMEN WHO ARE NOT WORKING THAT day gather at the White Horse or the Ideal or the International for beer and conversation. The executives and business lunchers from the industries just to the west throng the Dorgene restaurant and the Lion's Head coffee house; meat-market workers and communications scientists fill the bakery lunchroom. Character dancers come on, a strange old man with strings of old shoes over his shoulders, motor-scooter riders with big beards and girl friends who bounce on the back of the scooters and wear their hair long in front of their faces as well as behind, drunks who follow the advice of the Hat Council and are always turned out in hats, but not hats the Council would approve. Mr. Lacey, the locksmith, shuts up his shop for a while and goes to exchange the time of day with Mr. Slube at the cigar store. . . .

THE BABY CARRIAGES COME OUT, AND clusters of everyone from toddlers with dolls to teenagers with homework gather at the stoops. When I get home after work, the ballet is reaching its crescendo. This is the time of roller skates and stilts and tricycles, and games in the lee of the stoop with bottletops and plastic cowboys; this is the time of bundles and packages, zigzagging from the drug store to the fruit stand and back over to the butcher's;

this is the time when teenagers, all dressed up, are pausing to ask if their slips show or their collars look right; this is the time when beautiful girls get out of MG's; this is the time when the fire engines go through; this is the time when anybody you know around Hudson Street will go by.

AS DARKNESS THICKENS AND MR. HALPERT moors the laundry cart to the cellar door again, the ballet goes on under lights, eddying back and forth but intensifying at the bright spotlight pools of Joe's sidewalk pizza dispensary, the bars, the delicatessen, the restaurant, and the drug store. The night workers stop now at the delicatessen, to pick up salami and a container of milk. Things have settled down for the evening but the street and its ballet have not come to a stop. I know the deep night ballet and its seasons best from waking long after midnight to tend a baby and, sitting in the dark, seeing the shadows and hearing the sounds of the sidewalk. . . .

PEOPLE WHO KNOW WELL SUCH ANIMATED city streets will know how it is. I am afraid people who do not will always have it a little wrong in their heads – like the old prints of rhinoceroses made from travelers' descriptions of rhinoceroses. On Hudson Street . . . we are the lucky possessors of a city order that makes it relatively simple to keep the peace because there are plenty of eyes on the street. But there is nothing simple about that order itself, or the bewildering number of components that go into it. Most of those components are specialized in one way or another. They unite in their joint effect upon the sidewalk, which is not specialized in the least. That is its strength. ➤

Source: *The Death and Life of Great American Cities* (Random House, 1961), 50–54.

City of Clubs

CLARE COFFEY

At a time when sociologists warn of an epidemic of loneliness, a native Philadelphian celebrates her hometown's patchwork of clubs – the tiny communities that give a city zest and color. Clubs won't save the world, or your soul. But what would life be without places for joining together in human fellowship?

WHEN I WAS YOUNGER and broker, a day spent wandering around Philadelphia was entertainment enough. Window shopping around Rittenhouse Square or Jeweler's Row was fine. Better yet were an hour or two wandering from Rittenhouse Square to Society Hill, over to Old City and down to Pennsport, on residential streets without commercial attractions. The stately stone façades of Walnut Street and the snug brick walls of Catharine Street posed an endlessly tantalizing question – what lay behind them? The question became more pressing in the unexpected delight of a gate that perhaps concealed a garden. And best of all were windows: deep, dark pools of possibility, from the depths of which a cat, plant, statue, or silhouette might swim to the surface.

A residential city street seemed something like C. S. Lewis's wood between the worlds: a traveling place, with portals to a thousand smaller worlds contained therein. I wanted to get inside and know each of them, and at the same time to stay on the city street looking in, suspended on the threshold of uncertainty and speculation.

Even sweeter was when some seeming domicile turned out to have some formal social structure attached to it – a little placard hanging over the door, or a bronze plaque on the wall. THE RAVEN LOUNGE or THE

Clare Coffey is a writer living in Moscow, Idaho.

AMERICAN THEOSOPHICAL SOCIETY conjured up new dimensions of possibility.

These were clubs, places where public persons secreted themselves away and made themselves private, without retreating to the full unselfconscious opacity of a domestic house. Philadelphia is a city of clubs, Sandy Smith told me over scotch, and as he is the city's premier real estate journalist, he's the man to know. The metropolitan club grew out of the eighteenth-century coffee house, E. Digby Baltzell tells us in *Philadelphia Gentlemen,* a 1950s ethnography of Philadelphia's upper class. There's the Junto, of course, Ben Franklin's self-improvement and everyday philosophy society. Eighteenth- and nineteenth-century fire brigades, too, presaged modern fraternal organizations; they were as much mutual aid and brawling societies as they were public safety apparata. In *Governed by a Spirit of Opposition,* Jessica Choppin Roney contends that voluntary and civic associations provided a way for ordinary citizens of a strati-fied and fragmented city to participate in direct political action and control.

> ## Philadelphia is a small town disguised as a big city.

But the root of the phenomenon may lie deeper. "Philadelphia," Smith told me, "is a small town disguised as a big city." Whether a too abrupt separation from the village green and its small-scale society set early Philadel-phians in patterns of over-compensation, or whether something in the water just turns Philadelphians into ferocious little partisans of their subcultural territories, the feedback loop is now firmly established.

I talked to Smith in the Pen and Pencil, one of Philly's Center City clubs. But unlike most of its storied WASP fortresses, the Pen and Pencil possesses a distinctly raffish charm – perhaps appropriate for the nation's oldest press club in daily operation. Framed by a brick archway and a wrought-iron grille, a neon "P & P" casts its glow out onto Latimer Street. If you're a member, you can let yourself in. If you're not, you can rap on the door and hope the bartender hears. The bartender is less harried than most; an elderly man in a waiter's uniform, he says it's a good union job. He's been here a long time.

Inside, it's all vinyl tabletops and ashtrays around the well-stocked bar. Big stories by famous members hang on the wall. When it gets late, you can help yourself to a hot dog from the boiler. It's a place for members to sit and work, to grab a quiet drink or smoke of a late afternoon, to meet Larry Krasner for an off-the-record Q and A.

Because it's a private club, it can stay open past two in the morning. This has given rise to a somewhat dichotomous membership. It's formally a club for working journalists. After hours, it's informally a club for area bartenders, waiters, and hospitality workers. Late at night, a concierge from one of the city's most presti-gious private clubs stops by to blow off steam; little worlds and the worlds that they're built on tangling up at the root system level.

The only downtown club with half as much going on is the Vidocq Society, where a membership limited to law enforcement veterans, scientists, and psychologists solve cold cases together. They don't respond to my request for comment, afraid, I choose to believe, that I'd out-Marple them all.

Most of the other clubs around Rittenhouse Square tend to have pedigree. The Philadelphia Club serves as the final threshold to upper class society, according to *Philadelphia Gentlemen.* The Acorn and Cosmopolitan Clubs are women's equivalents, where wives of Biddles, Cadwaladers, and Morrises lunched in the days when proper society did not dine out publicly.

The Franklin Inn is a little different. It

is certainly pedigreed, founded in 1902 and boasting Howard Pyle, N. C. Wyeth, and E. Digby Baltzell himself among its members. Its home is a beautiful colonial revival on South Camac, whose interior has the slightly creaky deliciousness of an old house, perfectly furnished and under-renovated. It hosts impeccable lunches. But while it is and was functionally upper class, the first criterion for membership has always been active participation in or appreciation of the city's arts and letters scene. And the Franklin Inn prides itself on cultivating a convivially bellicose ethos.

In the same neighborhood lies the Stotesbury Mansion, a magnificent carved stone and wrought iron gilded-age townhouse. In 1925, after all the usual storied-gilded-age-townhouse history, including a cop-diverting mirror maze built during prohibition, the mansion fell into the hands of the Catholic Philopatrian Literary Institute. The "Philo" was formed during the worst anti-Catholic nativist years for the purpose of demonstrating that the Irish could read and love America just as well as anyone else, thank you very much. There must be at least seven or eight different Irish clubs and fraternal organizations in Philadelphia; they range from "nominally ethnic darts league" to "transatlantic Sinn Féin fundraising committee." My grandfather was in three or four. My brothers joined Roman Catholic High School's Ancient Order of Hibernians division. But the Philo has the best real estate.

The city-block-sized second empire building occupied by the Union League is, to my partisan eye, less beautiful than the Philo. But it is probably grander, and certainly bigger. The inside stretches on and on, sweeping marble staircase after sweeping marble staircase, leather armchair after leather armchair, bronze bust after bronze bust. True to its political origins – formed in 1862 to support the Union

Army and Republican endeavors – it remains a place for movers and shakers in Philadelphia. Around the 1890s the League let in too many new millionaires for it to belong to the Philadelphia Club's rarefied heights, but still,

if you want to be somebody in Philadelphia, you should probably spend some time at the Union League.

These fine distinctions of upper-classness were unknown to me before beginning this project, and they conjure up a dreary vision of club life: the possibility of endless knocking on yet another exclusive door. It raises the question: Is there something unwholesome about clubs themselves? Is the unselfconscious opacity of the domestic or the open-ended activity of the street (on my way to the League I had to hurry by an SEIU rally and an impromptu open-air bachata lesson) preferable? To escape the miasma and the question let us turn our attention to another set of clubs united around a common objective: the Mummers.

Give Us Whiskey, Give Us Gin

Mummers clubs lie largely in South Philadelphia. But the Aqua String Band clubhouse is

The Union League Club, where the Vidocq Society holds their meetings

in Bridesburg, a working-class neighborhood of single-family homes in the northeast part of the city. Aqua members don't necessarily live in Bridesburg, but the clubhouse is an important part of the neighborhood. They hand out candy on Halloween and host "beef and beers" for the nearby Polonia Club's beneficial association.

Inside the clubhouse is a small room with a bar at one end. When I arrived, a small orchestra waited in an open space at the front. Accordions, banjos, saxophones, violins, and drums sat assembled for rehearsal, as did their players. High school students in backwards baseball caps and jerseys; businessmen and firefighters in their thirties, forties, and fifties; and a young and serious salesman for Knights of Columbus insurance were in various stages of goofing around before practice.

Not all of the club's members are in the band. To be in the band you have to know how to play – high school orchestras are a prime recruiting ground. Or at least you have to be able to learn, because the Aqua String Band is nothing if not democratic. This is a point that the captain, Ken Maminski, impressed on me as one of the biggest misunderstandings about the Mummers.

"People think it's some sort of secret society, that you need to know somebody to get in," he said over a beer in the clubhouse back garden. "That's not true. We're always looking for new members, always ready to welcome somebody new. I know in about ten minutes of talking to someone whether he'll be a good fit in the clubhouse, and if he is, we'll find a place for him."

There are in fact a thousand places for someone who wants to be in the Aqua String Band, each requiring a different kind of skill or creative talent. There are set designers, set builders, and stage hands who keep everything moving on New Year's Day; dancers, choreographers, bandmasters, and music arrangers; logistical masterminds and accountants keeping track of it all. On New Year's Day everyone has a role to play, but there's no distinction within the clubhouse.

What are the Mummers? There are two answers.

The first is that the Mummers are an association of independent clubs, divided into Wench brigades, Comics, Fancies, Fancy Brigades, and String Bands, who stage competitive performances every year in an official New Year's Day parade in Philadelphia. Mummers go back to the city's colonial era, when immigrants from Scandinavia, Great Britain, and Ireland brought over the curious old-world custom of costumed house visits and plays around Christmastime. They'd celebrate New Year's Day by shooting off guns and greeting householders with the rhyme:

> Here we stand before your door,
> As we stood the year before;
> Give us whiskey; give us gin,
> Open the door and let us in.
> Or give us something nice and hot
> Like a steaming hot bowl of pepper pot.

Even then, Mummers were known for being rowdy; the city tried to outlaw them once, to little effect. Finally, in 1901, under the sound principle that if you can't beat 'em, organize 'em, it launched the first annual Mummers Parade, with judging and prize money.

The other answer is a memory: wrapped in a scratchy wool blanket, hoisted on my dad's shoulders, jammed into the crowd lining both sides of Broad Street in the biting cold of January. As I remember, it went like this: people jostling, laughing, drinking out of only semi-discreet containers, watched the Mummers strutting down the street. First came the Wenches, burly construction workers with painted faces and flounced skirts and golden slippers (sneakers spray painted gold) twirling parasols; then the Comics and their skits; next the Fancies, unrecognizable and resplendent in sequins and feathers dyed jewel tones, enormous headdresses, like some strange bird-gods from afar. And then came the String Bands, playing the familiar songs – "Oh, Dem Golden Slippers," "When You're Smiling," "I'm Looking Over a Four Leaf Clover" – marching up the street toward the judging station, where they would break into elaborate song and dance routines under the judges' critical eyes.

The January winds could blow as they liked. A new year was being born, in sequins and color and strings, in the relentless, buoyant, jangling, overwhelming spectacle, and in the incorrigible Mummers' strut.

The January winds could blow as they liked. A new year was being born, in sequins and color and strings.

What goes into all this spectacle? A year's worth of time and effort and money, it turns out.

Unlike the New Orleans Mardi Gras Day Parade or the Macy's Thanksgiving Day Parade in New York, the Mummers Parade has no official sponsorship beyond the city's prize money. All costs are borne by the respective Mummers clubs – the suits are designed in-house and manufactured by a specialty costume maker. All those sequins and feathers can come to the price of a small house. To raise the money, string bands perform all over the country, traveling to gigs by bus.

But before any of this can happen, themes must be proposed to the theme committee. A theme is debated, discussed, tinkered with, perfected – sometimes for several years – before its adoption. In 2018, the theme was "Lights Out," a riff on *Monsters, Inc.* After the committee officially votes on a theme, it's time to figure out how to make it a reality. The captain's son showed me a software program he uses to model the set and placement transitions for each part of the performance. Across the street, in the rec center, Mrs. Maminski is teaching the dancers her choreography. (The Aqua club is formally all male but functionally a family clubhouse; various other clubs are co-ed. Since it's easy to

Performer at the Clef Club, November 2019

join the club that suits your preferences, there seems little contention over it.)

The club's nature as family affair is fortunate, given the amount of time it demands. Maminski was ready to retire, in fact, until his son expressed interest in joining. Now all four Maminskis argue over the dinner table about how a dance should go, where a group should be placed, or which part of the arrangement should come first.

Nor is the Maminskis' all-consuming interest in perfecting the performance unique to them. After practice, the band hangs around, ordering pizza and watching "mum tapes" – recordings of previous performances. They can identify a misstep, a particular performer underneath layers of face paint and costuming, a particular area where they've improved. "It's so creative," one member told me when I asked what he gets out of these long Tuesday nights. He's right.

Drill down far enough in your quest to understand the Mummers, and you get to the pure performer, who makes and acts because that is what humans do.

Excellence in this arena doesn't need much further rationalization. And the Aqua club is pursuing excellence, steadily rising through the rankings bestowed by the Mummers Parade judges every year.

The Mummers are fiercely competitive. Maminski has friends and relatives in various other clubs, he said, "except on New Year's Day." On New Year's Day you hope that everybody between you and first place falls down and sprains their ankle.

The Aqua club is home. "We're brothers," Maminski said. He likes knowing that if his son is going through something that's hard to share with dad, he can talk to the other guys at the club. He likes coming back to Bridesburg on New Year's Day, delirious with the post-parade high, and seeing the whole neighborhood turn out to welcome them. This year, he knows, they'll come back to Bridesburg with the trophy; this year's their year. I believe it.

The House That Jazz Built

The Mummers are not the only Philadelphia institution founded on a love for performance. The Clef Club, several blocks down from the Union League on South Broad, is informally known as "the house that jazz built." In the 1930s, when black musicians had a hard time finding a place in white unions, musician Frankie Fairfax organized Local 274 for them, under the auspices of the American Federation of Musicians. Local 274 also had a performance space and social club for entertainers to relax, enjoy their craft, and meet other musicians; this space eventually became known as the Clef

Club. John Coltrane, Dizzy Gillespie, and Nina Simone were just a few of its famous members.

In the 1960s, desegregation of the unions became a federal mandate. Unfortunately, this often meant that black unions were assimilated into white ones, losing their charters, their real estate, and their financial assets in the process. Local 274 resisted as long as it could, arguing in court that since, unlike the white unions, it had never discriminated by race, it had always been in fact an integrated club. It lost; but by spinning off the Clef Club as a separate entity, it was able to keep its assets, and more importantly, its independence.

Now the Clef Club is a jazz performance space with a strong musical education program. Lovett Hines, Clef's music education director, talks about young musicians who have come up through the club the way a proud grandfather talks about his children: remembering them all by name, showing you pictures, detailing every accolade they've earned. And they are an impressive bunch, playing everywhere from Carnegie Hall to Beyoncé's Super Bowl halftime performance. And when they come back to play at the club, the bar is there for them the way it was for Clara Ward and Philly Joe Jones – to relax, to reminisce, to get to know the up-and-comers in a new generation of Philadelphia jazz.

Farther down Broad Street, past where any respectable clubman would stray when the Union League was first built, sits a low, square brick building, wedged tightly between its neighbors on a residential street. There is nothing to indicate that this is not somebody's modest home, except the unobtrusive red neon lights over the transom: Filippo Palizzi Club. There is nothing to indicate that this is one of the most sought-after dinner seats in Philadelphia, except the line of people at five p.m. on a Thursday, quietly waiting for the doors to open.

South Philadelphia in its early days was home to the poor, the immigrant, and the tough customer. Now it is home to everyone: the post-college up-and-comer out for a good time, sharing a house with six of his friends; the girls I went to school with – Donnas, Giannas, Tinas, Reginas – their brothers at Roman Catholic High School for Boys, and their nonnas; the wealthy couples in Queen Village with four hundred grand to drop on a townhouse for themselves and two dogs; the sturdy pockets of Irish in Pennsport; the new immigrants whose status is yet untinted by rose-colored nostalgia. From the mid-nineteenth century onward, South Philly welcomed Italian and Irish immigrants en masse, as well as African Americans moving northward in the great migration. Lately it has welcomed Mexicans, Hondurans, Cambodians, and Vietnamese, to name only a few. Also lately it has welcomed – and not welcomed – gentrifiers. You can get a three-bedroom brick-row home in Lower Moyamensing for $175,000; new construction can go for $300,000. In Queen Village, where South Philadelphia kisses Society Hill and Center City, homes are going for four hundred to eight hundred grand.

All this is to say that South Philadelphia is changing and remaining. The prices go up, but a working family can still buy a home. Some families move out to the suburbs; others stay, and new ones move in. Expensive new construction has not overwhelmed the squat brick homes on tightly packed streets, and the skyline is still low and flat and netted with drooping wires. You can sample some of the

Families are liable to have a matriarch in the neighborhood whose Sunday gravy is the gravitational center of home.

most vaunted offerings in Philly's restaurant scene, or get a slice and a beer for under five bucks. Families stay in the neighborhood for a hundred years or for ten, bickering over

The iconic sign over the entrance of the Filippo Palizzi Club

parking and bringing each other Christmas cookies. In high school it was the best place to trick-or-treat for teenagers politely determined to get theirs, and I expect it still is.

Palizzi Club

Above all, what has remained is the sense of the place as an Italian-American holdout. Families who moved out to the suburbs are liable to have a matriarch in the neighborhood whose Sunday gravy is the gravitational center of home. Italian flags flutter on every corner. Whatever restaurants move in and out, the culinary base remains the same: roast pork sandwiches on Amoroso rolls, Cappucio's meats, DiBruno Brothers' fine grocery.

It is one of the curious dynamics of human self-narration that a national consciousness often emerges from or enforces the disintegration of more local identities. The "Italian character" of South Philly is something seen in retrospect, when time and assimilation

have both done their work. In fact, immigration was not from any generic Italia: it was primarily from specific towns within Abruzzo, Campania, and Sicily.

When the Palizzi Club first came into being, immigrants were so many and so recent that distinctions were possible on a microscopic level. The club was originally founded as a social hub and mutual aid society for neighborhood residents from the Abruzzan town of Vasto. (The club is named for one of Vasto's prominent citizens, a painter named Filippo Palizzi.)

"It was a social club," Joey Baldino told me on the phone, "but it was more than that. People took care of each other. If you got sick, if your house burned – the club would take care of you."

Mutual aid was an absolute necessity in those days, when recent immigrants faced both poverty and discrimination, and the church was run almost entirely by the neighborly but mistrusting Irish. Over the years, the club became something of a bellwether for the changes in South Philly. Mutual aid became less necessary, and the club began expanding its membership – from Vasto to Abruzzo, from Abruzzo to southern Italy, and from southern Italy to Italy, full stop.

The club remained a place for the neighborhood to meet, have a drink, or throw darts on Sunday after church. Eventually, its presidency and de facto proprietorship passed into Baldino's family. He remembers a childhood of celebrations within its walls. For first communions and birthdays, weddings and funerals, attendees would gather to celebrate or mourn in the long, narrow clubhouse at the glossy wooden bar which the club's first members inaugurated in 1918.

There are clubs like this all over Philadelphia and its suburbs, like the Palombaro Club of Ardmore, down the street from Carlino's Specialty Foods and Milano's Auto Repair,

Inside the
Palizzi Club

where on most summer days you can find
a few older men playing bocce in the little
courtyard, and a few more drinking Yuengling
or amaros in a conspicuously unrenovated
bar. Most weekends the hall will be rented out
for a wedding. They have never regained the
centrality and the prestige they had throughout
the first half of the twentieth century, but they
are important in the lives of the core they still
serve, and they hang on.

But what separates the Palizzi Club from
all these with whom it shares a common
background is an accident of history, or fate.
It's Joey Baldino.

Baldino is a celebrated chef and restaurateur. His main restaurant, Zeppoli, a
Collingswood, New Jersey homage to the
Sicilian food he grew up with, appears regularly on best-of lists in the greater Philadelphia
region and beyond. When word got out that he
was, as *Philadelphia* magazine put it, "opening
a members-only restaurant in Philadelphia," so

many people flooded the new applicants' site
that it temporarily shut down.

But it's not quite accurate to say that
Baldino was "opening" a members-only
"restaurant." He did not revive the club after
long disuse, nor acquire and design it as a
concept. He took it on as a family trust.

When Baldino's uncle, the club's then-
president, fell ill, he had two choices: shut the
club down, or pass it on to a new generation.
He asked Joey if he'd like to take over. Joey
accepted. He redid the electrical and plumbing,
filled the menu with family recipes and
the bar with a judicious selection of classic
cocktails and imported amaros, and opened
up an otherwise unchanged clubhouse to new
membership. The response has been overwhelming, and perhaps at times bemusing.

Media coverage has described the Palizzi
Club as a "speakeasy-style restaurant" but, "It's
not a speakeasy. It's not a concept," Baldino
said. The club's much-noticed decor is not

perfectly executed mid-century modern; it's just the place he remembers as a kid at a moment when fifties paneling and vinyl happened to be in fashion. The deceptively homey façade and quiet residential location aren't there to manufacture a mystery, but because they always have been. Concepts are projected outward onto the public; Baldino's gambit aims, tentatively, to draw people into a private vision.

"It's always been a neighborhood club, and that's what I want it to be. Only now the neighborhood is hipsters as well as the old-timers." So Palizzi caters to them both.

Palizzi's famously strict rules are in place to keep it functioning primarily as a social club, not a hot spot. Cash only, dress nice, no phones out, no pictures, keep it down for the neighbors, no reviewing. Members enforce the rules amongst themselves, Guido Martelli, the head waiter, told me. "We have a lot of members here who are regulars."

They'll come in on a quiet Sunday and hang out at the bar, both original club members and neighborhood residents who joined when Baldino opened up membership. They'll nudge someone and tell them to put their phone away if necessary. "The club means a lot to people, and they want to keep it the way it is," Martelli said.

This was also the rationale for closing new membership when the club proved more popular than Baldino could have imagined. Of course, exclusivity enforced with sincerity is kerosene poured on the fires of public demand. It's easy to imagine a cynical story, with a chef at home enough in two different worlds to arrange a calculated marriage. But talking to Baldino, it's impossible to think that's the correct read. You can hear the love in his voice, the pride in the popularity of his family's club, the eagerness to keep its traditions alive; most tellingly, you can hear a small note of care, that having opened up something so personal to a wider public, he might find it misread, misunderstood, misused.

It's a delicate situation: to persist through another century, the club would have to change, and it's a piece of stunning good fortune that a restaurateur of Baldino's caliber was ready in the wings. But Baldino's gifts come with the dangers of celebrity; the rules, the rituals, and the limits are a way of managing that danger, of threading the needle between oblivion and generic fashionability. If the Palizzi Club was a long-time bellwether for the changes in South Philly, it's now a palimpsest for Philadelphia as a whole; having weathered the dangers of disappearing entirely into the past, it's now trying to avoid disappearing entirely into the future.

> You can hear the love in Baldino's voice, the pride in the popularity of his family's club, the eagerness to keep its traditions alive.

I think it's succeeding, but I won't tell you precisely why. That would be too much like a review, and I promised not to review. And I will admit, with a bit of a brag, that when I took my leave there was a membership card waiting for me, stamped with the Vasto crest. It will be there for me when I next come home – to Philadelphia, to the small town pretending to be a big city, to the worlds within worlds, to my city of clubs. ⤳

THOSE WINTER SUNDAYS

by ROBERT HAYDEN   drawings by JULIAN PETERS

SUNDAYS TOO MY FATHER GOT UP EARLY

AND PUT HIS CLOTHES ON
IN THE BLUEBLACK COLD,

THEN WITH CRACKED HANDS THAT ACHED
FROM LABOR IN THE WEEKDAY WEATHER MADE

Julian Peters is an illustrator and comic book artist living in Montreal, Canada, who focuses on adapting classical poems into graphic art. This visual interpretation is taken from Peters's upcoming collection Poems to See By *(Plough, 2020).* plough.com/poemstoseeby

I'D WAKE AND HEAR THE COLD SPLINTERING, BREAKING.

WHEN THE ROOMS WERE WARM, HE'D CALL,

AND SLOWLY I WOULD RISE AND DRESS,

FEARING THE CHRONIC ANGERS OF THAT HOUSE,

SPEAKING INDIFFERENTLY TO HIM,

WHO HAD DRIVEN OUT THE COLD

Save Your Sympathy

A review of *This City Is Killing Me: Community Trauma and Toxic Stress in Urban America* by Jonathan Foiles

JOHN THORNTON JR.

Brian Peterson, *left to right: Ruby, John, James and Charley*

IF "THE PERSONAL IS POLITICAL," then so is the psychological. That was the discovery of Jonathan Foiles, a therapist at a mental health clinic in Chicago. When in training to become a social worker, he found that his favorite aspect of the job was helping homeless clients – so when, in graduate school, he had to choose between a mental health and a policy track, he picked the one that seemed to offer that same individualized opportunity to make a difference.

But in his years of experience at the clinic, he came to realize that this focus on individuals can obscure clear thinking about the historical and political conditions that harm people not only physically but also mentally and psychologically. As he puts it, "We diagnose individuals, not cultures or neighborhoods, with depression." His new book – called, in an apparent nod to Chicago bluesmaster Dusty Brown, *This City Is Killing Me* – is his attempt to bring the two tracks together.

Foiles wants readers to see the ways in which mental illness resembles other illnesses: outside factors matter. Just as contaminated water increases the risk of cancer, the instability of unsafe housing can increase the risk of depression, anxiety, or post-traumatic stress disorder. When dealing with the hardships of life, family breakdowns, assaults, homelessness,

---

John Thornton Jr. is the pastor of Jubilee Baptist Church in Chapel Hill, North Carolina.

or addiction, it matters whom you go home to and also where you live, why you live there, who profits off it, and who makes decisions about your home's value or lack thereof. Education matters, and so does the quality of the school; the kids and parents who rely on that school are usually the least able to determine its quality or whether it stays open.

In each chapter of the book, Foiles writes about his work with an individual client. Jacqueline, his first transgender patient, struggles with borderline personality disorder while dealing with social rejection and the habitual dangers transgender people face. A single mother named Frida had her children removed from her care by the Department of Child and Family Services (DCFS) for neglect. Robert suffers with PTSD after an abusive upbringing in a dangerous and dilapidated low-income housing complex. Luis hoards and demonstrates obsessive behaviors driven by fear of loss. Anthony deals with the pain of losing his teenage son to gun violence.

Foiles is careful not to reduce his clients and their suffering strictly to the political; his respect for people as individuals shines through in his writing. While telling their stories, he pulls back to give a brief history of one of the material injustices he believes contributed to their need for mental health services. Jacqueline bounces from home to home while waiting to receive Social Security disability insurance. Frida, who never received the support that could have helped her take care of her children effectively, faces a confusing bureaucratic labyrinth in the DCFS, and the social workers assigned to her case frequently burn out only to be replaced by others with far too great a caseload. Robert not only has to deal with homelessness and the emotional scars of his childhood but also the lack of affordable housing in Chicago.

To emotionally protect himself from these compounding traumas, Robert has created a narrative of his childhood in which he was born a prince in Africa only to have kidnappers bring him to the United States. He harbors a deep suspicion of his own race and remains convinced that one of his neighbors wants to kill him. Foiles pieces together Robert's background: he grew up in the Cabrini-Green housing project in Chicago, one of the most dangerously violent before the city tore it down. In addition to the distress induced by this surrounding, he also believes that Robert faced a good deal of abuse in his childhood. As city services go, Robert fell through all the cracks.

Foiles takes this opportunity to tell the story of Cabrini-Green. He writes of its construction after World War II, its delicate balance between white and black that existed for years and eventually tipped as a result of white flight and closing factories. As the percentage of black residents rose, the average income dipped. Repairs stopped. Crime escalated. Even as the problems persisted, people wanted to live there, as Chicago, like pretty much all American cities, didn't have enough affordable housing. Eventually the city closed Cabrini-Green as part of the Chicago Housing Authority's 2000 Plan for Transformation. At the time, the mayor promised that the plan included provisions for the residents of low-income housing to transition into mixed-income residences. As of 2017, Foiles notes, fewer than 8 percent of the displaced households had made this transition. Meanwhile, there is a nice, new Target where

"It says something about the soul of a city that our leaders are willing to rob people of their homes to replace them with businesses."
Jonathan Foiles

the housing complex used to be. "It says something about the soul of a city that our leaders are willing to literally rob people of their homes to replace them with bright, shiny businesses," Foiles says.

WHILE READING THIS CHAPTER, I thought about the low-income housing directly across the street from a church I worked at in Winston-Salem, North Carolina. Constructed in the middle of downtown during the 1970s, Crystal Towers has about two hundred units reserved for elderly and disabled residents. The Housing Authority of Winston-Salem (HAWS) says the building needs about $7 million in repairs. The elevators often don't work. It is not a good place to live, but it's home for many who have lived there for years; its proximity to downtown means they can participate in the larger community without needing to drive, which many of them cannot.

> **When looking down on someone, we can't look up and see the forces that put them down there in the first place.**

Shortly before I left that church to start a new one, HAWS announced plans to sell Crystal Towers. With million-dollar condos just a block away, it became one of the most valuable pieces of property in the city, and because of federal regulations, HAWS can't operate at a financial loss. The director of HAWS has repeatedly said that all of the residents of Crystal Towers will wind up in comparable, stable housing. My guess is that this will have roughly the success rate that Chicago had in transitioning Cabrini-Green residents to mixed-income housing.

The church I worked at had a few members who lived in Crystal Towers. Most of the membership lived in far more opulent settings. About once a week we'd have someone from across the street come to us in need of rent money. I tried to help when I could, using the church's benevolence fund, but the scope of the problem far outweighed what just one church could do.

The standard approach to social action for both conservative and liberal Christians tends to center on sympathy, on sharing a feeling with another person suffering from poverty, racism, or other forms of inequality. I may not have the same experience as the residents of Crystal Towers, but I can find a time when I was rejected, a time when I worried about rent or paying my bills. This experience of sympathy, the thinking goes, will motivate me to reach out and help or push for change. Our church's proximity to Crystal Towers should have produced a good deal of sympathy and thus a good bit of action. It obviously didn't.

Foiles wants little to do with this attitude. He writes, "I do not want you to feel sorry for my clients. I don't feel sorry for them, and I don't think they would want anyone else's sympathy either. Sympathy does nothing to change their situation in life." We possess a wide range of ways to approach the suffering of others, from righteous indignation to tragic sorrow to humble admiration – but at bottom, these feelings do not matter. I think Foiles refuses sympathy because in situations of grave inequality, sympathy without condescension becomes incredibly difficult, if not impossible. When looking down on someone, we can't look up and see the forces that put them down there in the first place – the forces that would just as soon have put us there had things been a little different. Foiles writes, "I want you to see them, to be forced to confront the impact that policy decisions have upon the lives of our cities' poorest residents."

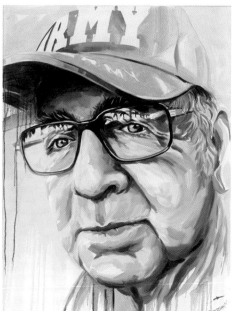

Brian Peterson, *left to right: River and Rebekah, Ben, Stevie*

Hannah Arendt once asked, "Should human beings be so shabby: that they are incapable of acting humanely unless spurred and as it were compelled by their own pain when they see others suffer?" I'm afraid the answer is that we are so shabby, that we are often incapable of acting humanely even when we do share another's pain. We are so shabby, but we don't have to be.

Compassion compels us to look for something that goes beyond the divides we live with. But if the personal and psychological are political, so are friendship and solidarity. We do not find a bridge across our class, racial, and political divides merely by discovering a mutual feeling of sorrow, but also by speaking about the world as it is and working together to build a better one.

FOILES PRODS US to move away from our interior states of sympathy, just as his own trajectory took him out of his clients' internal struggles to the facts of the world around them. A world of staggering inequality, in which condos can sell for millions of dollars to net a profit for an investor while people sleep on the sidewalks beneath. A world where the market economy seems to determine the value of every human life and everything we hold dear. A world in which people treat a government-owned building's disrepair and the violence in and around it almost as a natural disaster, something that is no one's fault and not the result of political decisions made by the powerful. He writes with a keen awareness that any Christian ought to have and that many often avoid: that while our struggles for happiness, community, peace of mind, and love draw us to something beyond the political, they also take us through it.

As Foiles shows, the patchwork of services to help these people is not nearly enough. More than individual progress in therapy or piecemeal acts of charity, what is needed is a robust social welfare system that includes universal healthcare, guaranteed housing, well-funded public schools, and humane social services. Greater financial equality and far fewer guns in circulation would also help. In this alternate universe, many of Foiles's patients – spared

Brian Peterson, *left to right: Crescent, Pam, Bahati*

their precipitating trauma – might never have developed symptoms at all. Those who did, he notes, would have had access to care much sooner and more productively. This would not be a world free of mental illness, but it is the right scale at which to think about it.

To achieve these goals, Foiles gestures toward Martin Luther King Jr.'s Economic Bill of Rights and Poor People's Campaign as ideas whose time has come again. All this sounds like a tall order, but as Christians we should aim even higher.

I find myself repeatedly drawn to the words of the socialist theologian Denys Turner: "Christianity will have proved its own truth in practice," he writes in a 1975 article for *New Blackfriars*, "when and only when the structures of domination, oppression, and exploitation, the structures of lies, mystification, and hate, the machinery of war, of imperialism, of racism . . . have been wiped from the face of the earth." Meanwhile, "Christ, love, community are present in the world, really present, in the form of

their absence, in the form, that is, of a real possibility . . . of love, of emancipation, of community." It is our responsibility to try to bring about that real possibility.

Of course, such a world may not come about in our lifetimes and Christians must continue living with the sufferings of Foiles's clients – sufferings we have limited resources to address and that many of us share.

What little we can do is care for one another in ways that expose the destruction into which our politics and economic system press us. Even if such a church is only a "gnat on the back of an elephant," as Eberhard Arnold, founder of the Bruderhof, once said, the calling remains. Heeding it means distributing our own goods, providing housing for the homeless, and caring for the elderly, and much more besides. But we shouldn't do this as a way for the wealthy and powerful to outsource these responsibilities. We must do this because we can and should, and hopefully others will choose to let go of their idolatrous commitments and join us. ⤙

Editors' Picks

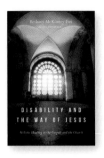

Disability and the Way of Jesus: Holistic Healing in the Gospels and the Church
Bethany McKinney Fox
(IVP Academic)

If God created each of us in his image, what does it mean to pray for healing for someone whom God made with a disability? How can the way Jesus healed guide churches today to truly become communities of inclusion for everyone? Acknowledging that misguided theology and healing ministries have often hurt more than helped people with disabilities and mental illness, Fox nevertheless believes a richer understanding of the gospel accounts of Jesus' healing ministry can provide an answer.

A seminary professor and pastor, Fox has also served people with disabilities in a L'Arche community. In this book, she combines perspectives from doctors, pastors, anthropologists, ethicists, and biblical scholars with personal experiences of Christians living with various disabilities.

With this range of voices, Fox helps us read the stories of Jesus in their cultural context and to recognize the biases of our own. A Western, individualistic, biomedical perspective focuses on the cure of a physical disease. But for Jews of Jesus' day, his miracles of healing are much more: they reveal God's power and presence. When his kingdom breaks in, not only do the blind see and the lame walk, but demons are cast out, sins forgiven, and formerly shunned people, whether lepers or sinners, are restored to their places at the table. Maybe those we have labeled and excluded are no more in need of healing than those of us who placed them there.

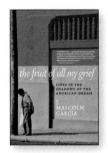

The Fruit of All My Grief: Lives in the Shadows of the American Dream
J. Malcolm Garcia
(Seven Stories)

The frontispiece quotes William Goyen: "My eyes often open up when I see a limping person going down the street. That person's wrestled with God, I think." That's how Garcia helps us see people in these haunting true stories of Americans living on the edge of survival: A trucker hauling drugs to pay for life-saving surgery for his son. An immigrant construction worker seeking sanctuary in a church, where he waits in limbo. Two sisters wrongly convicted of armed robbery, struggling to reenter society when they are finally set free after sixteen years in prison. A homeless-looking octogenarian who sleeps on the floor and gives away all his money to worthy causes. A Marine corporal, battling his own demons, on a road trip to check up on each of his men who made it home from Iraq.

Garcia delves into the inner lives of his subjects, channeling each person's distinctive voice, unfiltered. We can hope the fruit of all this grief, now shared, will evoke not just outrage but also empathy and compassion.

Inconspicuous Consumption: The Environmental Impact You Don't Know You Have
Tatiana Schlossberg
(Grand Central)

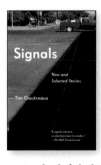

Most of us know we should be doing more about climate change. But what? Many books on the topic emphasize science and policy, blaming the biggest offenders and leaving our future in the hands of governments and corporations that have the power, but not the will, to effect change.

Several new titles make it personal, focusing on practical choices we can each make to reduce our footprint. While the intent is ostensibly to empower, to help us escape that feeling of helplessness, some seem more intent on spoiling our pleasure in the occasional bacon double cheeseburger.

On balance, Schlossberg succeeds in leaving the reader more hopeful than helpless, more stirred than shamed. A reporter rather than an expert, she skims across four areas directly related to our habits: technology, food, clothes, and fuel. Everyone will learn something. Did you know the electricity needed to power the internet contributes more carbon emissions than global air traffic, or that about a third of household electric use is by appliances in sleep mode? She calls out cows, of course (it's cow burps, not farts: 95 percent burps, 5 percent farts), but also the industrialization of crop farming, and the appalling fact that a third of food produced is never eaten.

Knowing the environmental impact of our consumption is a first step toward change. In a world where those least responsible are most affected, that is a matter of loving our neighbors as ourselves. But reading between the lines, it remains clear that personal change, while right and good, will never be enough. It will take more than better consumers to turn this tide. Together we will have to envision and create a society and economy that make it possible for everyone to live lightly on the land.

Signals: New and Selected Stories
Tim Gautreaux
(Knopf)

It's not every day you discover an unheralded master of the short story. Most of Gautreaux's are set in the left-behind towns of his beloved Louisiana Delta, a tough place to live and make a living. His characters are gritty and intriguing: a junk dealer, a childless exterminator, a typewriter repairman, a cook who "died and went to Vegas," a brain-damaged priest.

Then there's Mrs. Arceneaux, whose would-be thief made the mistake of trying to "rob me like the government." Mrs. Arceneaux and her five decrepit neighbors foil the thief with someone's double-barreled shotgun and her own top dental plate.

But such rough edges are suddenly backlit by redemption if someone turns that way. Before he is busted for DUI, an incompetent priest hears a confession that frees a soul, but the reader suspects the priest's own soul is better off for his hilarious bungling of a good deed.

Stories like these can make us better neighbors, reminding us of the inherent dignity and goodness in even the most undignified people, just waiting to be drawn out. ⇌ *The Editors*

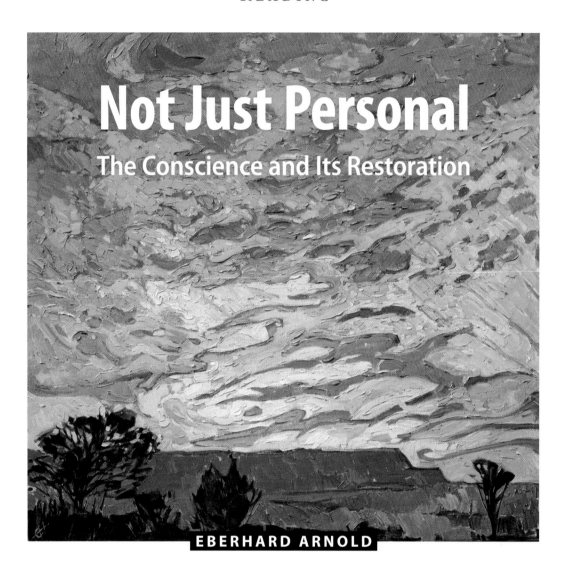

Not Just Personal
The Conscience and Its Restoration

EBERHARD ARNOLD

In 1932, in the waning days of the Weimar Republic, Plough's *founding editor, Eberhard Arnold, published a booklet on the conscience and its relation to politics and society. This article is adapted from a newly released English edition of that work.*

THE CONSCIENCE IS AN ORGAN of extraordinary delicacy, representing the deepest feelings of the human spirit. Like a sensitive recording instrument, influenced by every change of weather, it is liable to be damaged by any shock. When we thoughtlessly leave the doors of our inner life open to the ever-changing atmosphere of the times, the conscience is in danger of being thrown off balance.

But not only then: it can be led astray just as much by mental and intellectual development. Even an increase of religious activity can cause serious derangement. The conscience is an uncertain factor even in the holiest spheres of life. It remains diseased as long as it is not

Erin Hanson, *Desert in Color*

healed by the power of Jesus' surrendered life. Bound to false ideals, that is, to erroneous human thinking, it remains unreliable until it experiences freedom – and asserts its freedom – in the true and vital Word of God, in the living Spirit of Jesus Christ.

The unhealthy state of an erring conscience comes to expression in annihilating self-accusations, which can even lead to derangement. Here, the conscience is reacting in the wrong place. It is typical of all false ideals and goals that they rob the conscience of certainty about the essential thing, binding it instead to what is secondary. As long as other points of attraction compete with the magnetic pole, the compass needle jerks unsteadily here and there without any accuracy.

The conscience must be directed toward the kingdom of God.

This restlessness gives rise to a wavering judgment which, like a bird of prey, looks for a victim. There are cases in which a sick conscience lets no thought arise and no step be taken without submitting it to serious misgivings and harsh judgments. Such a sickness fills the whole of life with grievances and dissatisfaction, with self-laceration and injustice.

Only when the conscience that inflicts such suffering on itself experiences the remission of sins through Christ can healing be given. Those who have been forgiven much love much. Those who experience love forgive much.

HISTORICALLY, THERE WAS a tendency to call even the healthiest reactions of the conscience a sign of sickness that should be ignored, and this same tendency prevails again today in a new form. It must be repudiated decisively. The conscience must never be silenced or despised. Rather, it must be led to splendid health by being freed from false aims and directed toward the kingdom of God. In this way, it will be filled with new clarity and new content, leading to lively activity in all areas of life embraced by the conscience – not just in personal life, but in questions of public responsibility and vocational activity.

This purification includes being freed from property, bloodshed, and lying just as much as being purified in the area of sex. During and after the [First] World War, all manner of dishonest business practices gained ground, even in circles that had long shown a certain sureness of moral instinct. For much of the German nation, any effective defense the conscience might have had against the powers of hell had been destroyed – for example, by political murder (justified as "self-defense") and by thoughtless openness to allowing a recurrence of war and civil war.

Today again, there is scarcely any real uneasiness about the injustice of mammon and property – an injustice that in fact kills love in all aspects of life. In the obvious confusion of conscience among people, it is not surprising to find a lack of restraint over covetous desires and brazen infidelities. This critical and turbulent state is bound to lead to destruction; ominous signs gather on all sides. Meanwhile, spiritual leaders explain the ever-increasing confusion in such bedazzling ways that no one feels uneasy.

IN CHRIST, THE CONSCIENCE that used to be our enemy becomes our friend. Previously, it had to condemn our life; now it says yes to the new life given to us in Christ. Freed from all impurity through community with him, the human spirit accepts the assurance and certainty given in Jesus Christ. So the conscience, as Christ's conscience, becomes a representative of God.

The way of Jesus is love, agape. This kind of love is unique. It gives a very definite direction. It is a way, and this way is very clearly marked out. In the experience of God's love, Jesus Christ leads us up to the loftiest peaks of willpower, clarity of recognition, and a strength of heart that is joy. He does not do this for our sake. He wants us to pass on the streams of this power of love that is poured into our hearts. These streams are meant to flood the earth, revealing God's heart and establishing his glory.

Love gives up all possessions. Christ's justice conducts no lawsuits. It does not carry on a middleman's business or any business that is to the disadvantage of another. It foregoes all its own advantage, it sacrifices every privilege, and it never defends a right. Christ's justice never sits on a jury, never deprives anyone of freedom, and never passes a death sentence. It knows no enemies and fights no one. It does not go to war with any nation or kill any human being.

And yet when this justice is at work, it is justice in its most active form, peace in its most energetic form, and constructiveness in its most effective form. The sum total of all we are commanded to do is to love: to love with a pure heart, a clear conscience, and a genuine faith. In order for perfect love to flow freely, Jesus showed the conscience the way of responsible community in God. This is the essential nature of his kingdom and his church. ⤳

Adapted from The Conscience *(Plough, 2019), volume 2 of Arnold's masterwork* Inner Land. *Plough will publish the three additional volumes next year. Learn more at* plough.com/innerland.

The Inner Life
Volume 1

The Conscience
Volume 2

Experiencing God
Volume 3

Fire and Spirit
Volume 4

The Living Word
Volume 5

Inner Land
A Guide into the Heart of the Gospel
Eberhard Arnold

"Inner Land calls men and women to a life of such trust in God that their attitudes toward his kingdom, other people, material wealth, and earthly power are transformed."
Christianity Today

"Arnold's writing has all the simple, luminous, direct vision into things that I have come to associate with his name."
Thomas Merton

www.plough.com/innerland

(Continued from page 9)

Beauchamp raises good points in defense of his first thesis. The rise of "PMSCs" (private military security companies) remains unknown to many Americans. The privatization of combat which Beauchamp refers to correlates to the post–Cold War period, the vast if perhaps only momentary conquest of the world by liberal capitalism with its deregulation and moral decapitation. All of this suggests important moral, political, and pragmatic questions, most of which don't rise to the level of public scrutiny because of Americans' ignorance of the entanglement of war and profit-seeking.

But the soldiers do know. Many of them, like Beauchamp, serve alongside contractors, most of whom make five-figure monthly salaries. Though armed, they are not soldiers' brothers-in-arms. The veterans I've spoken with hold these men in contempt. Unlike Beauchamp, they intuit Augustine's point about the difference between fighting for greed and fighting for honor. Augustine calls greed a baser instinct; honor, while not the same as fighting for the true Good, is a superior motivation. Beauchamp can draw consolation from that: there is something different between fighting for money and fighting for even a corrupted state.

Joseph Capizzi, Washington, DC

I was disturbed to find the article "Mercenaries out of the Gate" by Scott Beauchamp in your Anabaptist magazine. While we all can share Mr. Beauchamp's concern and disgust with the use of the military to further the goals of capitalist corporations, his view of what is honorable should be offensive to the Christian reader. He writes, "To fight for one's nation as a soldier was honorable. To fight only for money became the ultimate mark of dishonor." When did it become acceptable, or even honorable, to kill? And is it honorable to kill for a flag, but not for a dollar? Did God say, "Thou shalt not kill, except if you're told to by your president"? Did Jesus say, "Love your enemy, but it is honorable to kill them"? Far too many of our Anabaptist forebears were hunted down and martyred by military men doing what they were instructed to do. Was that killing "honorable" because they were doing it for their nation? I share Mr. Beauchamp's concern about the use of mercenaries, but I have that same concern about anyone who kills people for any reason. None of it is honorable.

David Brown Kinloch, Louisville, Kentucky

Around the same time Scott Beauchamp was pulling tower guard as a soldier at one of the city-sized bases around Baghdad watching the Blackwater and KBR contractors come and go in their armored SUVs, wraparound Oakley glasses, and tactical khaki pants, I was stationed on a base in southern Iraq interacting with a different sort of military contractor.

My unit's mission was providing security for civilian supply trucks. With two up-armored HMMWVs in the front and two in the rear, we escorted long convoys of civilian trucks; big 18-wheelers like the kind you'd see in the States, twenty or thirty in a row, driving the length of Iraq's highways, with us American soldiers providing security: getting blown up and ambushed to ensure safe delivery of grape soda, frozen crab legs, construction supplies, diesel fuel, and monster energy drinks – all the materiel of war that kept the bases buzzing in their eerily domesticated bureaucratic routine, and supplied the combat units outside the wire, where only a minority of the troops ever ventured, with the fuel – both diesel and monster energy drinks – that kept them fighting.

Most of the contractors I interacted with on those missions weren't ex-US-military like those Beauchamp describes. There were a few of those guys driving the lead vehicles, the ones with armor plating, but the rest of the trucks were driven by a different kind of mercenary: men from Bangladesh, Turkey, Sri Lanka, other countries with no connection to the war, grouped together under the acronym TCN: "Third Country Nationals." The TCNs drove the refrigerated trucks full of food and the tankers full of fuel. They got blown up and maimed and killed all the time, pieces of them left on the roads of Iraq. Even when people talk about the rise of private contractor armies in the war on terror, you rarely ever hear about the TCNs. Their role in the war, like their deaths, doesn't take up much space in official histories or in the critiques of military privatization that focus on more notorious and symbolically potent groups like Blackwater. The TCNs were all over Iraq but they were hardly even there. They died without names.

I don't bring this up to disagree with Beauchamp's well-informed account of private military contractors. Where Beauchamp writes: "Capitalism and the military want, for lack of a better term, the same things. Both want intrusive intelligence and data gathering for purposes of control," I agree. But the control exists as a degraded replacement for a true purpose. The only rightful goal of war is peace; when that is discarded war becomes a profit unto itself. And while one form of control is the monopoly of valuable information, another form is the power to declare what counts as valuable and what's just surplus. With one hand the surveillance state collects; with another, it discards.

It's been a little more than ten years since I left Iraq and half as many years since the war officially ended and nobody ever asks me about the TCNs. How can you talk about people without names? *Jacob Siegel, New York City*

Scott Beauchamp responds: D. H. Lawrence wrote in "The Bad Side of Books" that "One writes . . . to some mysterious presence in the air. If that presence were not there, and one thought of even a single solitary actual reader, the paper would remain forever white." That's why it's always such a joy to receive thoughtful responses from my interlocutors. It's humbling to have proof that actual communication is happening.

Of course I remember the people Jacob Siegel mentions, the Third Country Nationals cooking our food and doing our laundry. During my second deployment, a regular soccer game developed between the Ugandan guards who manned the gates and the Eastern European sanitation workers. Whatever social or material advantage we had as Americans was erased on the playing field. And I remember a specific Sri Lankan man working in the base laundry who was always eager to quiz me on English vocabulary words he was learning. We once argued over the proper use of "void" and he won. As mysterious as the story of American soldiers is to their fellow citizens, the TCNs present an even more profound silence. They deserve a book all their own. And I think Siegel is the man to write it.

The distinction which Joseph Capizzi draws between the lures of money and honor is a fascinating one, and one which I recognize. Its spirit, quite obviously, suffuses the piece which I wrote. But David Brown Kinloch is also correct, I think, in his estimation of martial honor in light of the meaning of the cross. I was not a Christian when I went to war. I am now. As I grow in my faith, I count myself blessed to have voices such as Kinloch's reminding me to orient myself always towards the one supreme Good which cuts straight through the parsing of all the lesser ones. ➤

Madeleine Delbrêl

JASON LANDSEL

IN 1933, twenty-nine-year-old Madeleine Delbrêl moved with two friends to a house in Ivry-sur-Seine, a Paris suburb that was then a hotbed of Communism. They vowed themselves to a life of simplicity, chastity, and evangelism. Their plan was, simply, to love their neighbors – personally, affectionately, practically. She worked as a writer and lecturer, and sought every day to respond to those whom God set before her to love and serve.

On the streets of Ivry, Christians and Communists clashed openly, but the Delbrêl house had an open door, a place of hospitality where anyone from any background would be welcomed and accepted: "a tiny cell of the Church," Delbrêl wrote, "born in our time, making its home in our time."

She had not been raised as a Christian; her parents were fashionable agnostics. At seventeen, she wrote a manifesto beginning, "God is dead. . . . Long live death!" The Delbrêls held lavish parties; Madeleine entertained guests with readings. She studied philosophy at the Sorbonne, designed her own clothing, and cut her hair short. She became engaged to a philosopher, another atheist.

Then things fell apart. Her parents became estranged, and her fiancé broke off the engagement to join a Dominican order. Shattered, Madeleine's thoughts returned to the God question. "I met several Christians," she wrote, "neither older nor dumber nor more idealistic than I was; in other words, they lived the same life I did, they discussed as much as I did, they danced as much as I did."

And then, "I decided to pray. . . . By reading and reflecting, I found God; but by praying, I believed God found me and that he is living reality, and that we can love him the way we love a person."

Her conversion was conclusive – "bedazzling," in her words – and, from the age of twenty until the day she died, she never ceased being "overwhelmed by God."

Though she now rejected the Marxist material analysis of the world, she refused to reject the Communists themselves. "If there are Christian women whose husbands or children . . . are Communists," she wrote, "they love them with a love God makes his own. To love them, they don't have to accept the Party card that declares their opposition to God. . . . But by refusing their card, these women aren't required to deny their flesh, their heart, their affection."

Madeleine Delbrêl died working at her desk in Ivry-sur-Seine on October 13, 1964, from a brain hemorrhage; it was two weeks before her sixtieth birthday. In 2018, Pope Francis declared her "venerable," putting her on the path toward canonization as a saint.

"There are some people," she once wrote, "whom God takes and sets apart. There are others he leaves among the crowd, people he does not 'withdraw from the world. . . .' They love the door that opens onto the street. . . . We, the ordinary people of the streets, believe with all our might that this street, this world, where God has placed us, is our place of holiness." ⮞

Jason Landsel is the artist for Plough's *"Forerunners" series, including the painting opposite.*